NCFE

LEVEL 1/2 TECHNICAL AWARD

# BUSINESS AND ENTERPRISE

Tess Bayley
Leanna Oliver

HODDER
EDUCATION
AN HACHETTE UK COMPANY

Orders: please contact Hachette UK Distribution, Hely Hutchinson Centre, Milton Road, Didcot, Oxfordshire, OX11 7HH. Telephone: +44 (0)1235 827827. Email education@hachette.co.uk Lines are open from 9 a.m. to 5 p.m., Monday to Friday. You can also order through our website: www.hoddereducation.co.uk

ISBN: 9781510456785

© Tess Bayley and Leanna Oliver 2019

First published in 2019 by
Hodder Education,
An Hachette UK Company
Carmelite House
50 Victoria Embankment
London EC4Y 0DZ
www.hoddereducation.co.uk

Impression number 10 9 8 7 6 5 4 3 2

Year 2023 2022 2021

Cover photo © Shannon Fagan - stock.adobe.com

Illustrations by Aptara

Typeset in India

Printed in India

A catalogue record for this title is available from the British Library.

# Contents

Introduction to NCFE Level 1/2 Technical Award Business and Enterprise    iv

How to use this book    v

Acknowledgements    vi

## Unit 01 Introduction to business and enterprise

LO1: Understand entrepreneurship, business organisation and the importance of stakeholders    2

LO2: Understand the marketing mix, market research, market types and orientation types    25

LO3: Understand operations management    55

LO4: Understand internal influences on business    60

LO5: Understand external influences on business    72

Assessment practice    78

## Unit 02 Understanding resources for business and enterprise planning

LO1: Understand research, resource planning and growth for business and enterprise    82

LO2: Understand human resource requirements for a business start-up    99

LO3: Understand sources of enterprise funding and business finance    117

LO4: Understand business and enterprise planning    144

Assessment practice    157

Glossary    159

Answers to Test yourself questions    162

Index    170

# Introduction to NCFE Level 1/2 Technical Award Business and Enterprise

This book has been written to help you to master the skills, knowledge and understanding you need for the NCFE Level 1/2 Technical Award Business and Enterprise.

Throughout the course you will learn how to understand:

- entrepreneurial characteristics and business aims and objectives
- legal structures, organisational structures and stakeholder engagement
- the marketing mix, market research, market types and orientation types
- operations management
- internal and external influences on business
- research, resource planning and growth for business
- human resource requirements for a business start-up
- sources of enterprise funding and business finance
- business and enterprise planning.

The book is divided into two units.

## Unit 01 Introduction to business and enterprise

This unit gives you an understanding of what it means to be an entrepreneur and how businesses are organised. It will give you a knowledge of marketing, operations management and the influences that affect businesses.

## Unit 02 Understanding resources for business and enterprise planning

This unit looks at business planning, including research, resource planning and growth. It will help you develop knowledge of human resources and finance and how they support business and enterprise planning.

## Summary of assessment

The table below summarises how you will be assessed for NCFE Level 1/2 Technical Award Business and Enterprise.

| Component | Assessment type | Time | Percentage of qualification |
|---|---|---|---|
| Unit 01 Introduction to business and enterprise | Written examination | 1 hour 30 minutes | 40% |
| Unit 02 Understanding resources for business and enterprise planning | Synoptic project | 21 hours of supervised time | 60% |

# How to use this book

This book is designed to help you develop the knowledge, understanding and practical skills you will need during the NCFE Level 1/2 Technical Award in Business and Enterprise qualification. The features shown below appear throughout the book to support your learning.

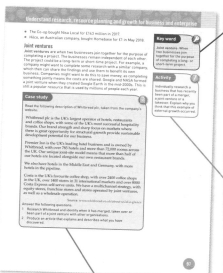

**Key words:** Definitions for important terminology are included throughout.

**Learning outcomes:** The learning outcomes for each unit are clearly listed, so students know exactly what to expect.

**Activities:** Students are encouraged to take their understanding one step further with short activities throughout.

**Remember:** A bullet summary of the key points appears at the end of each topic, to help students remember the most important aspects and to help them with revision.

**Case studies:** Examples of how different concepts might apply to a business.

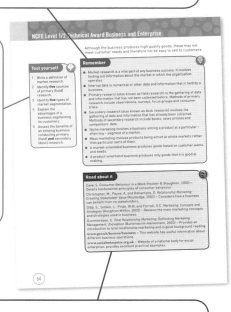

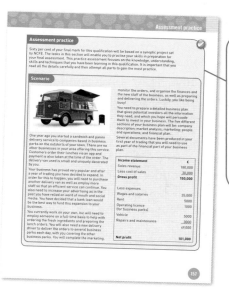

**Test yourself:** Questions are included at the end of each topic so students can test their knowledge and understanding of the content.

**Assessment practice:** Sample questions and activities to help you prepare for assessment.

**Read about it:** A list of books, websites and other sources of useful information can be found at the end of each learning outcome.

# Acknowledgements

The Publishers would like to thank the following for permission to reproduce copyright material.

## Picture credits

**p. 1** © Gorodenkoff/stock.adobe.com; **p. 5** © Sabinezia/stock.adobe.com; **p. 17** © devteev/stock.adobe.com; **p. 20** © TungCheung/stock.adobe.com; **p. 26** © Sergio Azenha / Alamy Stock Photo; **p. 28** © Brian Jackson/stock.adobe.com; **p. 32** t © Grzegorz Czapski/Shutterstock.com; b © Jonathan Weiss / Alamy Stock Photo; **p. 38** used by permission of Burnley FC; **p. 40** © Innocent Drinks; **p. 41** © Art Directors & TRIP / Alamy Stock P; **p. 43** © xy/stock.adobe.com; **p. 47** © JackF.stock.adobe.com; **p. 48** © Kaspars Grinvalds/stock.adobe.com; **p. 49** © Chris Brunskill/Getty Images; **p. 52** © kritchanut/stock.adobe.com; **p. 58** © Alterfalter/stock.adobe.com; **p. 61** © Rawpixel.com/stock.adobe.com; **p. 64** © Photographee.eu/stock.adobe.com; **p. 68** © Rainer/stock.adobe.com; **p. 81** © everythingpossible/stock.adobe.com; **p. 83** t BedHead shampoo © razorpix / Alamy Stock Photo; m © Roman Tiraspolsky/123RF; b © Buzz Pictures / Alamy Stock Photo; **p. 84** © nitikornfotolia/stock.adobe.com; **p. 85** © Photomika/stock.adobe.com; **p. 87** © wirojsid/stock.adobe.com; **p. 88** © Joshhh/stock.adobe.com; **p. 90** l © smuki/stock.adobe.com; m © Rtimages/stock.adobe.com; r © focusandblur/stock.adobe.com; b © EdNurg/stock.adobe.com; **p. 95** © peshkov/stock.adobe.com; **p. 96** © Jeff Bukowski/Shutterstock.com; **p. 100** © Egor/stock.adobe.com; **p. 106** © eccolo/stock.adobe.com; **p. 107** © SergeBertasiusPhotography/Shutterstock.com; **p. 112** © luckybusiness/stock.adobe.com; **p. 113** © mkos83/stock.adobe.com; **p. 118** © sumire8/stock.adobe.com; **p. 120** © Featureflash Photo Agency / Shutterstock.com; **p. 124** © laufer/stock.adobe.com; **p. 129** Reproduced with permission of tutor2u https://www.tutor2u.net/business/reference/breakeven-point; **p. 142** © maxandrew/stock.adobe.com; **p. 144** t © Rawpixel.com/stock.adobe.com; b © DOC RABE Media/stock.adobe.com; **p. 146** © kasto/stock.adobe.com; **p. 148** © Africa Studio/stock.adobe.com; **p. 150** © Nikolay Antonov/Shutterstock.com; **p. 153**; © Александр Беспалый/stock.adobe.com; **p. 157** © Alex Kondratenko/stock.adobe.com.

## Text credits

**p. 91** 'No tills? Now that is smart' by Ruth Sunderland, The Mail on Sunday: 12/08/2018. Reprinted with permission; **pp. 97–98** Reproduced with permission of Whitbread plc; **pp. 110–111** Learning and Development Case Study: Heinz – A training scheme full of beans by Mary Carmichael, HR Magazine, January 25, 2010. Reprinted with permission of Mark Allen Group.

Every effort has been made to trace all copyright holders, but if any have been inadvertently overlooked, the Publishers will be pleased to make the necessary arrangements at the first opportunity. Although every effort has been made to ensure that website addresses are correct at time of going to press, Hodder Education cannot be held responsible for the content of any website mentioned in this book. It is sometimes possible to find a relocated web page by typing in the address of the home page for a website in the URL window of your browser.

# Unit 01

# Introduction to business and enterprise

## About this unit

In this unit you will learn about:

- how to become a successful entrepreneur, considering different types of businesses that can be opened and how interested parties affect different organisations
- how different businesses market their products to the general public

- how different organisations operate within businesses and how organisations make their products
- how businesses provide effective customer service to their consumers
- the different factors that influence businesses and the internal and external factors that influence organisations.

## Learning outcomes

This unit is divided into five learning outcomes:

1 Understand entrepreneurship, business organisation and the importance of stakeholders.
2 Understand the marketing mix, market research, market types and orientation types.
3 Understand operations management.
4 Understand internal influences on business.
5 Understand external influences on business.

## How will I be assessed?

This unit is assessed by a written exam.

# Learning outcome 1: Understand entrepreneurship, business organisation and the importance of stakeholders

## 1.1 Entrepreneur

### 1.1.1 Being an entrepreneur

Being an **entrepreneur** is a skill. An entrepreneur is often described as a risk-taking individual, but there are a number of other aspects to becoming an entrepreneur.

Entrepreneurs are individuals who spot a gap in a market, develop a business idea and are willing to take risks in order to make the idea a reality. These individuals are usually highly motivated to succeed. There are three key motivators that drive an entrepreneur:

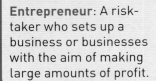

**Key word**

**Entrepreneur:** A risk-taker who sets up a business or businesses with the aim of making large amounts of profit.

- financial motivators
- personal motivators
- social motivators.

It is usually assumed that the key motivator for any entrepreneur is money. Entrepreneurs tend to want to earn high profits, buy luxury cars and spend many weeks on extravagant holidays. In recent years, however, a number of entrepreneurs have run a business not in order to make massive profits; instead, they have done it in order to meet their personal and social goals.

Entrepreneurs may decide to go into business for a number of reasons, for example:

- to have flexibility in their working life. Entrepreneurs often want to choose their own hours of work, set their own deadlines and have more control over their time
- to satisfy their desire to be their own boss and set their own rules
- to help people by producing products or services that will improve people's lives
- to create jobs in the local area and help the economy
- to learn new skills
- to be able to give something back to other people, for example, many successful entrepreneurs will donate time or money to worthy causes.

## Financial motivators

Many new businesses fail within the first few years. For this reason, the first financial objective is to survive. If an organisation is not viable, it is likely to run out of cash very quickly.

To ensure survival, an entrepreneur needs to ensure that:

- there is sufficient cash to pay business debts
- the business has access to sufficient sources of finance
- the organisation has a business model that is viable in the long-term.

Once the business's initial survival has been secured, an entrepreneur will turn to making a profit. This is when an organisation's revenue exceeds its total costs. In return for the risk and hard work put into the business, the entrepreneur will desire high profits over a long period of time.

The financial motivator for some entrepreneurs may be personal wealth. They may aim not just to earn an adequate income, but instead to gain a substantial personal wealth.

## Personal motivators

Profit is not the main motivator for setting up in business for a number of entrepreneurs. These individuals may be motivated by the desire for control over their working life, the opportunity to work from home or the option to combine work with family life. In recent years, a number of individuals have set up businesses after losing their job or after failing to secure promotion. Such individuals often feel that their skills are undervalued and they are not reaching their full potential. Other people become bored with being told what they have to do every day and so want to become their own boss.

## Social motivators

Some individuals feel a need to interact with and be accepted by others. These people may have a desire to escape from a boring or uninteresting job or have an intense desire to pursue one of their interests or hobbies. A key social motivator is the feeling of needing to gain personal satisfaction from building a successful business.

## 1.1.2 Entrepreneurial characteristics and skills

The characteristics and skills that an entrepreneur must have include:

- **A willingness to take risks:** Any new business venture carries risk, regardless of how carefully planned and researched the business idea is. A successful entrepreneur will be willing to invest large amounts of money and time into their ideas, while being fully aware that customers may reject the project and that it could ultimately fail.
- **An ability to undertake new ventures:** Entrepreneurs usually have vast amounts of imagination to identify business opportunities that will fill gaps in the current marketplace.
- **A desire to show enthusiasm and the initiative to make things happen:** Entrepreneurs do not wait for something to happen. They show determination, drive and energy to launch the new business. They take active roles in all aspects of the business initially to ensure its success.
- **Resources and funding:** These will be needed to make the investment to set up a business. For more on funding, see Unit 02 Section 3.1.1.
- **Time and commitment:** An entrepreneur needs to be able to understand and calculate the risks of and potential rewards from any venture.
- **The ability to invent and innovate: Invention** involves the making of new items. Inventors design and make products that are not currently available for sale, for example James Dyson and the bagless vacuum cleaner. Entrepreneurs then need the **innovation** to bring these new ideas to the market.

> **Key words**
>
> **Invention:** The creation of new items.
>
> **Innovation:** Bringing new ideas to the market.

In recent years, the role of the entrepreneur has been highlighted by television programmes such as the BBC's *Dragons' Den* and *The Apprentice*. These programmes highlight the characteristics and skills required to become an effective entrepreneur.

In order to be a successful entrepreneur, an individual needs to have the courage to be different. This will ensure that their business idea stands out in the market.

The following characteristics are often also seen in successful entrepreneurs:

- **Confidence:** In order to be successful, an entrepreneur needs to be confident to present their idea to the public. They will be able to show certainty and forcefully present their ideas.
- **Motivation:** The late Apple founder Steve Jobs said 'I'm convinced that about half of what separates the successful entrepreneurs from the non-successful ones is pure perseverance.' Entrepreneurs are passionate about their business ideas, therefore they are motivated to work long hours to ensure their business organisation is a success.
- **Determination:** An entrepreneur needs to be determined and decisive. In their own business, an entrepreneur will need to know what has to be done and not hesitate when making decisions.

- **Focus:** Entrepreneurs need to have a clear focus on their end goal. In most business organisations entrepreneurs will be focused on increasing sales, becoming a market leader, having high profits, etc.
- **Initiative:** Entrepreneurs often set up their business from a new idea. They are usually keen to think 'outside of the box' and use their initiative to do and try things before other people. Richard Branson said 'I've gone into business, not to make money, but because I think I can do it better than it's been done elsewhere. And, quite often, just out of personal frustration about the way it's been done by other people.'
- **Decisiveness:** An entrepreneur needs to be able to make important and often difficult decisions. They cannot be afraid to make decisions that may upset other people, for example, staff may need to be made redundant in order for a business organisation to succeed.
- **Analytical ability:** An entrepreneur needs to be able to gather and review a wide range of information. As part of this the entrepreneur needs to be able to see a problem from different points of view. By reviewing the different points of view, an entrepreneur should be able to solve their business problems.
- **Strong communication skills:** An entrepreneur needs to be able to communicate with a wide range of different people. In many cases they will need to be persuasive to ensure that the other person will listen to them.

**Dare to be different.**

**Figure 1.1.1** A successful entrepreneur needs the courage to be different

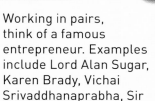
**Activity**

Working in pairs, think of a famous entrepreneur. Examples include Lord Alan Sugar, Karen Brady, Vichai Srivaddhanaprabha, Sir James Dyson.

Produce a poster that highlights the characteristics and skills that you think have made your chosen entrepreneur successful.

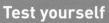
**Remember**

- Any new venture carries risks.
- Entrepreneurs must accept that their business ideas may fail.
- Invention and innovation are often linked.
- An entrepreneur is usually successful if they spot a gap in the market.
- A wide range of different skills are required to become an entrepreneur.

**Test yourself**

1 Write a definition of entrepreneur.
2 Explain the difference between invention and innovation.
3 Discuss the skills and attributes that an entrepreneur requires to be successful.
4 Explain how the phrase 'courage to be different' relates to an entrepreneur.

## 1.2 | Business aims and objectives

### 1.2.1 Financial aims and objectives

The aim of most businesses is to make a profit. However, there are a small number of organisations, such as charities, that exist to provide a service and are classified as not-for-profit organisations – sports clubs, for example, may be non-profit-making and exist to provide services to their members.

A new business will struggle to make a profit in its first few years of trading, therefore new organisations usually aim to break even.

### Break-even point

In order to set appropriate financial aims and objectives, the owner needs to review the business costs and revenues. Costs are expenses that organisations incur when producing and selling their products and services. There are a number of different ways of categorising these costs:

- **Fixed costs** remain unchanged when the output of a business changes, such as rent, loan repayments, advertising, salaries.
- **Variable costs** vary directly with the level of output, such as stock, raw materials and packaging costs.
- **Total costs** are the fixed costs plus the variable costs.
- **Revenue** is the money that a business earns from selling its goods or services.
- **Total revenue** is the selling price of the goods that a business sells, multiplied by the number of goods sold.

You can read more about these different types of costs and revenues in Unit 2 Section 3.2.2.

Many businesses want to maximise the profits they make. A **profit** is a financial gain. It is calculated as the difference between total revenue and total costs.

Business owners need to remember that there is always the possibility the organisation will not make a profit. For example, new businesses, small organisations and those struggling within a difficult economic environment may find it difficult to generate any profits at all. In these cases, a business may simply aim to break even.

### Key word

**Profit**: A financial gain. It is calculated as the difference between the total revenue and total costs.

### Stretch activity

Carry out internet research to investigate a business that has appeared in the news as failing to make any profit.

Discuss, in small groups, the business's strategies for increasing its profit.

## Definition of break-even

**Break-even** is the level of output at which total costs equal total revenue. At this point, a business is making no profit and no loss.

An organisation is able to calculate the number of sales it needs to make in order to break even each year, known as its break-even point. A number of assumptions have to be made when a business calculates its break-even point:

- All output that has been made is sold.
- No inventory is left unsold.
- Only one type of product is made by the business.
- All costs are categorised as either fixed costs or variable costs.

## Break-even formula

The break-even formula is:

$$\text{Break-even point (in units)} = \frac{\text{Fixed costs}}{\text{Selling price per unit} - \text{Variable cost per unit}}$$

**Contribution** is the amount left over after variable costs have been taken away from sales revenue. Contribution per unit is calculated as selling price per unit less variable cost per unit. This means that the break-even formula can also be written as:

$$\text{Break-even point (in units)} = \frac{\text{Fixed costs}}{\text{Contribution per unit}}$$

Contribution is different to profit, as fixed costs are not taken away from the selling price.

## Activity

Complete the following table to calculate contribution per unit and break-even point in units.

The first row has been completed as an example.

| Total fixed costs (£) | Selling price per unit (£) | Variable costs per unit (£) | Contribution per unit (£) | Break-even point |
|---|---|---|---|---|
| 60,000 | 20 | 10 | 20 – 10 = 10 | 60,000 / 10 = 6000 units |
| 240,000 | 100 | 60 | | |
| 600,000 | 25 | 15 | | |
| 500,000 | 36 | 11 | | |
| 3,000,000 | 250 | 150 | | |
| 500,000 | 500 | 300 | | |
| 500,000 | 300 | 200 | | |
| 300,000 | 250 | 150 | | |
| 300,000 | 150 | 50 | | |
| 900,000 | 450 | 200 | | |

## Case study

Snuffie Dog Apparel sells luxury dog collars and leads.

Answer the following question:

1  The owner, Phil, has prepared the following table of costs based on varying levels of output. He has asked if you can help him work out the missing figures. The first line has been completed as an example.

| Output of collars and leads (units) | Variable cost per collar and lead (£) | Total variable costs (£) | Total fixed costs (£) | Total costs (£) |
|---|---|---|---|---|
| 20,000 | 5 | 100,000 (20,000 × 5) | 250,000 | 350,000 (100,000 + 250,000) |
| 30,000 | 5 | | 250,000 | |
| 50,000 | 5 | | 250,000 | |
| 75,000 | 3 | | 250,000 | |
| 90,000 | | 270,000 | 250,000 | |
| 100,000 | 2.50 | | | |
| 150,000 | | | 250,000 | |

### How break-even information is used

Break-even information is used by a business to determine how many units it needs to sell in order to cover its costs and not make a loss. Accountants may use this information to see how different sales levels will affect an organisation's profits. By determining how much needs to be sold, targets can be set for sales people.

When launching a new business or trying to secure finance, the owner may calculate break-even information in order to persuade a bank to lend their organisation money. Break-even information can form part of a business plan.

## Profitability

As we have already considered, most businesses exist to make a profit. Profit is the owners' reward for investing in the business.

### How profit per unit is calculated

Businesses often want to know how much profit a particular product or service is making. This can be calculated as:

**Profit or loss per unit = Selling price per unit − Total costs per unit**

(Remember: **Total costs per unit = Fixed costs per unit + Variable costs per unit.**)

### How profit is calculated for a given level of output

In general, profit is calculated for a given level of output as:

**Profit or loss = Sales revenue − Total costs**

## Cash flow

**Cash flow** is the movement of money into and out of a business. Cash comes into a business in the form of receipts. Receipts could be from taking out a loan or mortgage or from selling goods to its customers; these are known as cash inflows.

Cash goes out of a business in the form of payments. Payments could include wages, salaries, utilities, raw materials, etc.; these are known as cash outflows.

Net cash flow is calculated as:

$$\textbf{Net cash flow = Cash inflow – Cash outflow}$$

Cash flow is different to profit as cash flow relates only to money coming into and out of a business, whereas the calculation of total profit includes other items.

**Key word**

**Cash flow:** The movement of money into and out of a business.

# Increasing revenue and profit maximisation

Over time, businesses need to ensure that they are able to increase their revenue and also maximise the profit they make. In order to increase revenue and maximise profit, businesses will:

- raise their prices once they have entered the market
- up-sell their products, for example a car dealer will sell a car and then make every effort to encourage the customer to also purchase luxury accessories
- cross-sell, where a business sells one product and then makes every effort to sell an additional product at the same time, for example financial institutions often try to get individuals to take out a credit card when opening a bank account
- offer bundle offers, where organisations offer customers a set of products to buy together, for example when selling a bed a retailer may offer a bundle of bed, mattress, head board and bed covers
- increase their marketing and advertising to ensure they are noticed by the public
- offer discounts to customers who buy large quantities and/or buy on a regular basis
- host special events, for example launch events for new cars.

## 1.2.2 Non-financial aims and objectives

Non-financial aims and objectives are those that help improve a business as a whole.

When opening a business, an entrepreneur will prepare a detailed business plan that contains the organisation's aims and objectives. The main non-financial aims and objectives of a business include:

- customer satisfaction
- expansion
- employee engagement/satisfaction
- diversification
- ethical/corporate responsibility.

### Customer satisfaction

The majority of businesses exist in part to ensure that they make their customers happy. After visiting different organisations, people are often asked to comment on the service they were offered. In recent years, there has been an increase in the number of online surveys requesting information about customer service and customer satisfaction. If a business has satisfied its customers, they are more likely to return to the business, become loyal to the organisation, spend more money at the business and recommend it to their family and friends. Online review sites provide a means for customers to express their opinions on businesses. For example, TripAdvisor allows travellers to comment on hotels, tours, restaurants, etc. and to show both the organisation and other people how satisfied they were with the business.

### Expansion

If a business runs out of cash, it would not be able to pay for its inventory or pay its workers and would be classed as insolvent. The owners would either have to raise additional money or cease trading and close down the business.

To prevent this from happening, businesses carefully monitor their cash flow, usually on a weekly or monthly basis, to ensure they have sufficient money to pay their debts. They will often plan ahead by preparing a cash flow forecast and identifying if additional finance is required.

Once a business has maintained a stable cash flow, it is able to consider expanding its operations. This may include purchasing new premises or employing new staff. In order to do this, the business must have sufficient money or funds to pay for the initial costs, for example the building, and also to pay the ongoing costs involved, for example the heating and lighting costs. Many businesses need to take out a mortgage or loan in order to expand (see Unit 2 Section 3.2.2). Successful expansion should mean that the business is able to make more sales and increase its profit levels.

## Employee engagement/satisfaction

Most businesses aim to have happy, satisfied employees. These employees provide excellent customer service, and work effectively and efficiently. It is often thought that satisfied employees will stay with the same employer and take very little time off work. This means that the business does not have to fund unnecessary sick pay, provide cover for absence or incur the costs of replacing staff.

## Diversification

Any organisation needs to find its place in the market and identify where its particular products or services fit alongside other businesses. In order to reduce the risk involved in operating in a market, businesses often spread their risk by expanding the range of products sold or services they offer.

Businesses sell a wide range of products and services to individuals, who are known as their customers. These customers are known as the **market** in which the business operates.

To enable a business to decide which products and services to offer, it may divide the market in which it operates into segments. The size of these segments may be measured in terms of the number of sales or the value of the sales. Not all segments are the same size: in Figure 1.1.2, for example, Market Segment 2 is approximately twice the size of Market Segment 1.

**Figure 1.1.2** Sizes of different market segments

Prior to diversifying, a business needs to decide in which **market segment** to offer its products/services. The particular market segment that a business plans to sell its products or services to is known as its **target market** and the business will produce goods and services to meet the needs of that particular segment. Once the business is successful in one market segment, it may then be able to expand into other segments.

There are a number of key reasons why businesses need to segment their markets. One key reason is that all customers are different and have unique needs, wants and aspirations. In general, customers vary because of the benefits they require, the amount of money they are able/willing to pay, the quantity of goods they require, the quality of goods they require, and the time and location at which they wish to purchase the goods.

### Benefits they require

Depending on their needs, different customers will require different products and services. For example, customers who live in warm countries such as Spain and Italy are likely to have less need for winter coats than individuals who live in colder countries such as Norway and Iceland.

## Key words

**Market**: A place where buyers and sellers come together to interact and exchange goods with each other.

**Customer/market segmentation**: The division of a market into groups or segments.

**Target market**: A particular group of customers at which a good or service is aimed.

### Amount of money they are able/willing to pay

Depending on household income, individuals usually have a set amount of money they budget to spend on goods and services. For example, individuals willing to pay a large sum of money for a holiday may book an exotic cruise, whereas a family with a limited budget may book a self-catering caravan holiday close to their home.

### Quantity of goods they require

Different customers require different quantities of goods. For instance, a family of five will need to purchase more food from the supermarket than a single person living on their own.

### Quality of goods they require

This often links to an individual's income. People with high incomes are more likely to purchase better quality goods than individuals on a low income. For example, a multi-millionaire may decide to purchase a new Rolls-Royce car, while a family on a low income may purchase a second-hand car that costs much less money.

### Time and location at which they wish to purchase the goods

The type of goods that a customer wishes to purchase will affect when and where the goods are purchased. For example, a person who needs a bottle of milk for breakfast is likely to go early in the morning to a store that is local to their home and buy the milk immediately. Individuals who are looking to purchase a new piece of furniture are more likely to be prepared to wait for their goods, to travel further to purchase those items, and to take time to consider the purchase before committing.

## Ethical/corporate responsibility

Businesses often see one of their responsibilities as being to operate ethically. This means that they consider social and environmental factors when completing their business operations. Two businesses that have strong ethical backgrounds are The Body Shop and the Co-op.

In order to consider a business's ethical and corporate responsibilities, it is important to consider to whom the organisation is responsible. The following table considers different ethical and corporate responsibilities.

**Table 1.1.1** A business's ethical and corporate responsibilities

| Individual or group of people to whom a business is responsible | Example of a business's responsibility |
|---|---|
| Investors or shareholders | To provide a good return for the money they have invested in the organisation. |
| Employees and managers | To ensure that they are paid a fair salary or wage and have safe and appropriate working conditions. |
| Customers | To provide good quality products at a fair price. |
| Suppliers | To purchase goods on a regular basis and to pay all their invoices on time. |
| Environmental groups | To reduce pollution and have environmentally friendly operations. |
| Local community | To provide employment for people living in the local area and also to ensure that the business's operations do not cause disruption, for example noise during the night. |

## Remember

- Businesses aim to break even in their early years.
- Business owners each have individual aims and objectives for their business.
- Businesses need to find their place in the market.
- Businesses aim to be market leaders and to have a large market share.
- Any business needs to retain its current customers.

## Test yourself

1 Write a definition of financial objectives.
2 Describe why a business would have non-financial objectives.
3 Write a definition of market segmentation.
4 List **three** non-financial aims for a business of your choice.
5 Write a definition of customer retention.

# 1.3 Structures

## 1.3.1 Legal structures

The economy can be divided into two main sectors:

- the public sector.
- the private sector

### The public sector

The public sector is made up of central government, local government, and businesses that are owned by the government. Over the last thirty or so years, the number of government-owned firms in the UK has shrunk massively. In 2019, very few examples remain; Royal Mail is one of the remaining public sector organisations.

### The private sector

The private sector includes businesses that are owned by private individuals. Businesses in the private sector include:

- sole traders
- private limited companies (Ltd)
- partnerships
- public limited companies (plc).

The different forms of ownership for business start-ups in the private sector, as well as their advantages and disadvantages, are outlined in the following table.

**Table 1.1.2** The different forms of ownership for business start-ups

| | Definition | Examples | Advantages | Disadvantages |
|---|---|---|---|---|
| **Sole trader** | A **sole trader** is a business that is owned and controlled by one individual. | Plumber or electrician working on their own. Mobile hairdresser or beauty therapist working on their own. | Easy to set up. Low set-up costs. The owner makes all of the business decisions, reducing the time taken to make a decision. Sole traders can choose their own working hours, holidays, etc. Limited legal requirements in relation to accounting, etc. | Difficult for the business to grow very large due to the amount of money available to the sole trader. Difficult for a business to grow as there is a limit on the amount of work one person can do on their own. The sole trader has no one to share responsibility or decisions with. The sole trader may have to work long hours and find it difficult to take holidays. A sole trader has **unlimited liability**. This means the sole trader would need to pay the business's debts if they could not be paid. |
| **Partnership (see also section on limited liability partnerships below)** | A **partnership** is a business that is owned and controlled by two or more individuals. In most cases, there are 2–20 partners, but this number can be exceeded for professional partnerships, e.g. accountants and solicitors. | Estate agents Accountants Solicitors Small/medium-sized retail stores | Greater capital investment available from the different partners. Partners bring different skills and attributes to the business. Responsibility and risk are shared among the partners. Partners can discuss queries before finalising decisions. Bigger public image than sole traders. | Decision-making can be time-consuming as all partners need to be consulted. There is potential for disagreement and conflict in decision-making. All partners are jointly responsible for the business debt – like sole traders, a partnership has unlimited liability. (All partners would need to pay the business's debts if they could not be paid.) |
| **Limited company** | A limited company is a business owned by shareholders and run on a day-to-day basis by directors. There are two types of limited company: private limited companies (Ltd) and public limited companies (plc). | Large public organisations, for example: <br>● Manchester United<br>● Asda<br>● Barclays<br>● BP | Greater capital investment available from the shareholders. Investors do not have to actively run the company. Bigger public image than sole traders and partnerships. **Limited liability**. | Costly and complicated to set up. Limited companies need to be registered with Companies House. Annual accounts need to be published. Investors and shareholders expect income in the form of annual dividends. Dividends are a share of the company's profits. There is the possibility of a takeover if enough shareholders try to purchase shares. |

| | Definition | Examples | Advantages | Disadvantages |
|---|---|---|---|---|
| **Franchise** | A **franchise** is a business where the franchisor (the owner of the business idea) grants a licence (the franchise) to another business (the franchisee), so they can sell its brand or business idea. The franchisor owns the business idea and decides how the business will be operated and run. | Well known franchise businesses include: <br>● McDonald's <br>● Pizza Hut <br>● Starbucks | Limited business and industry experience are required, as the business model already exists. <br>The franchisee owns the business but not the idea. <br>As the franchise is well known, it is easier to raise finance. <br>The franchisee benefits from the skills, advice and support of the franchisor. <br>It is easier to gain customers, as the brand is already well known and recognised. | The initial and on-going costs of operating a franchise are not cheap. <br>The franchisee needs to stick to the marketing activities agreed by the franchisor. <br>It may be difficult to break into a new area if competing with other franchisees. |
| **Co-operative** | An association of like-minded people who work together to meet their common economic, social and cultural desires. Co-operatives are owned by their staff, who are members of the firm. | There are three main types of co-operative: <br>● Consumer co-operatives, where members buy goods in bulk, sell to other members and divide the profits between members. <br>● Worker co-operatives, where workers buy the business and run it. <br>● Producer co-operatives, where producers organise the distribution and sale of products themselves. <br>Examples include: <br>● Co-operative Press <br>● People's Press Printing Society <br>● New Internationalist <br>● Brighton Energy Cooperative <br>● Edinburgh Bicycle Cooperative | The ownership, finance and control of a co-operative is in the hands of its members. <br>They exist for the benefit of their members. <br>Profits are shared among members. | Like profits, losses are shared among their members. |

## Key words

**Sole trader**: A business that is owned and controlled by one person.

**Unlimited liability**: When the business owners are personally liable for the debts of the business in the event that the business cannot pay them.

**Partnership**: A business that is owned and controlled by two or more individuals.

**Limited liability**: When the business owners are liable only up to the amount of money they have invested in the business.

**Franchise**: A business where the franchisor (the owner of the business idea) grants a licence (the franchise) to another business (the franchisee) to operate its brand or business idea.

### Private limited companies and public limited companies

Private limited companies (Ltd) can only sell their shares to family and friends, whereas public limited companies sell their shares on the open market to the general public.

Private limited companies are owned by between two and 50 shareholders. One of the most important things about a limited company is that the liability of the shareholders is limited. This means that limited companies have limited liabilities; the investors can only lose the money that they have invested. None of their personal possessions is at risk.

Public limited companies (plc) are owned by a minimum of two shareholders; there is no maximum number of shareholders. They have a separate legal identity – the company can sue and be sued. Public limited companies are more complex to set up and have a minimum share capital of £50,000.

### Limited liability partnerships

In a limited liability partnership, partners in the organisation are not personally liable for the business's debts if they cannot be paid. Each partner is liable only up to the amount of money they invested into the business. This is known as limited liability.

## Features of each form of business ownership

**Table 1.1.3** Features of each form of business ownership

| | Owners | Basic legal requirements to start the business | Liability? | Responsibility for decision-making | Distribution of profit to the owners | Funding |
|---|---|---|---|---|---|---|
| **Sole trader** | One business owner | The sole trader registers with HMRC to pay taxation on profits made. | Unlimited | Single owner | Single owner | Sole trader's money<br>Bank loan<br>Overdraft<br>Mortgage |
| **Partnership (unlimited liability)** | Two or more business owners | Each partner registers with HMRC to pay taxation on their share of the profits made.<br>A partnership agreement may be produced to identify the key role and responsibilities of each partner. This may include how profits/losses are shared. | Unlimited | All partners equally unless there is a partnership agreement that states differently. | All partners equally unless there is a partnership agreement that states differently. | Partners' personal money<br>Bank loan<br>Overdraft<br>Mortgage |
| **Limited liability partnerships** | Two or more business owners | Each partner registers with HMRC to pay taxation on their share of the profits made.<br>A partnership agreement may be produced to identify the key role and responsibilities of each partner. This may include how profits/losses are shared. | Limited | All partners equally unless there is a partnership agreement that states differently. | All partners equally unless there is a partnership agreement that states differently. | Partners' personal money<br>Bank loan<br>Overdraft<br>Mortgage |

| | Owners | Basic legal requirements to start the business | Liability? | Responsibility for decision-making | Distribution of profit to the owners | Funding |
|---|---|---|---|---|---|---|
| **Franchise** | The franchisor owns the business idea. The franchisee owns the right to use the business idea and the individual business that is set up. | The franchisee registers with HMRC to pay taxation on profits made. The franchisee needs to pay the agreed amount of money to the franchisor each year. | Varies depending on the franchise | The franchisor is responsible for overall decisions relating to the business design and idea. For example, store layout and brand logos, etc. The franchisee decides on working hours, holidays, etc. | The franchisee earns the profit from the franchise but needs to pay the annual fee and agreed profit percentage to the franchisor. | Franchisee's own money Bank loan Overdraft Mortgage |
| **Private limited company** | Shareholders (family and friends) | Documents need to be submitted to Companies House – Memorandum and Articles of Association. | Limited | Directors appointed by the shareholders to run the company on their behalf. | Via dividends | Shares from family and friends Loans |
| **Public limited company** | Shareholders (the general public) | Documents need to be submitted to Companies House – Memorandum and Articles of Association. | Limited | Directors appointed by the shareholders to run the company on their behalf. | Via dividends | Shares sold to the general public Loans |

## Activity

Barrie is planning to open a bakery business selling sandwiches, pies and cakes to local organisations. He is unsure of what type of business structure to choose.

Prepare a short report offering Barrie advice on his potential options.

## 1.3.2 Organisational structures

The organisational structure is the way in which a business is arranged to carry out its activities. This is illustrated in an organisational chart.

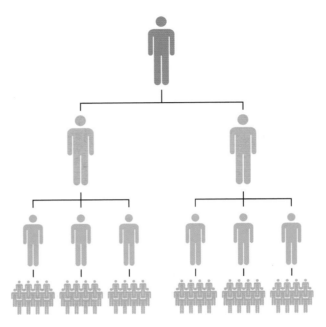

**Figure 1.1.3** An organisational chart

Businesses frequently change their organisational structures. Owners believe that changes are required in order to meet the demands of the current marketplace. Businesses need to compete with their competitors and organisational change often reduces costs and expenses.

### Levels of hierarchy

The hierarchy in a business refers to the number of layers of authority within the organisation. Usually, this is between the chief executive and the shop floor.

A business with many layers is known as a tall organisation, whereas when there are few layers the organisation is known as flat.

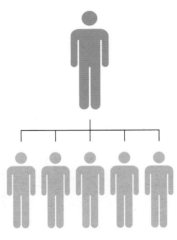

**Figure 1.1.4** A flat organisation

- A flat organisation may look like Figure 1.1.4. Flat organisations have wide spans of control as one manager is in charge of a large number of people.

- A tall organisation would be represented as in Figure 1.1.5. Tall organisational structures have narrow spans of control, meaning each person is responsible for only a small number of other people. This allows managers to keep close control over the work of the employees that they look after.

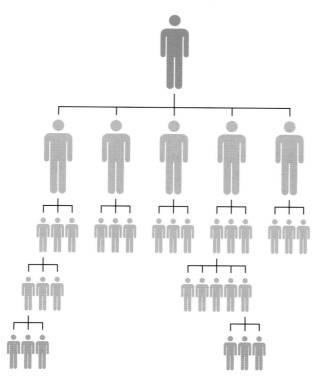

**Figure 1.1.5** A tall organisation

As the control widens in tall organisations, workers are likely to be able to operate with a higher degree of independence, as in flat structures. This is because it is impossible for a manager to closely monitor a larger number of people.

It is usual that a narrow span of control exists at the top of an organisation and a wider span of control exists at the bottom.

Traditionally, UK businesses have tended to be tall, with long **chains of command**. Due to the number of layers, communication is often difficult and decision-making can be very slow.

**Key word**

**Chain of command:** The line of communication and authority within a business.

### 1.3.3 Restructuring

During the life of a business, the organisation's structure may need to change. For example, a sole trader may decide to take on a partner to introduce additional capital and ideas in their business. Alternatively, a partnership may want to reduce their personal risk and therefore may turn the business into a private limited company. This would mean the partners would have limited liabilities and would become shareholders and directors.

### Delayering

Businesses may remove layers of authority as it allows faster and more effective communication. This is known as delayering. The idea was influenced by Japanese and American companies.

In recent years, many large business organisations have taken out their middle layer of managers. This has been due to pressures from the Far East requiring UK businesses to reduce costs. Many large companies have done this by reducing the number of layers in their organisational structure.

### Redundancies

If an organisation reduces the number of its workers, these workers need to be made redundant as there is no longer any work for them. The cost savings for the business are often very large. These workers are given redundancy payments but then need to find other employment.

Other forms of restructuring may affect the organisation of business areas within the firm. Business areas are covered in Section 4.2.

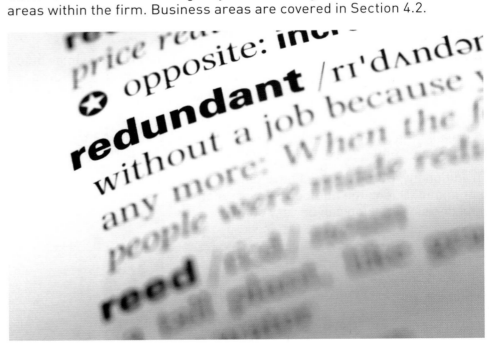

**Figure 1.1.6** Reducing the number of workers requires redundancies

## Case study

M.H. Lee is a self-employed painter and decorator. She has been in business for the last 15 years and has established a number of loyal and repeat customers.

To aid the efficiency of her business, she is considering forming a partnership with her friend Olson, who is a self-employed interior designer.

Answer the following question:

1 Discuss the potential benefits and drawbacks of M.H. Lee and Olson forming a partnership.

## Remember

- The public sector is made up of central government, local government, and businesses that are owned by government.
- The private sector includes businesses that are owned by private individuals.
- A sole trader is a business that is owned and controlled by one individual.
- A partnership is a business that is owned and controlled by two or more individuals.
- A limited company is a business that is owned by shareholders and run on a day-to-day basis by directors.
- A franchise is a business where the franchisor (the owner of the business idea) grants a licence (the franchise) to another business (the franchisee), so it can sell its brand or business idea.
- A co-operative is an association of like-minded people who work together to meet their common economic, social and cultural desires.

## Test yourself

1 Write a definition of franchise.
2 Explain the difference between a sole trader and a partnership.
3 Write a definition of unlimited liability.
4 Identify **three** sources of capital for a private limited company.
5 Describe the **three** main types of co-operative.

## 1.4 Stakeholder engagement

### 1.4.1 Internal stakeholders and 1.4.2 External stakeholders

A stakeholder is any individual who has an interest in a business. This may include individuals who will be impacted by a business's decisions. Stakeholders can include:

- individuals
- groups of people
- other organisations.

There are two main types of stakeholders:

- **Internal:** These are stakeholders within an organisation, for example owners, managers, employees and workers.
- **External:** These are stakeholders outside of an organisation, for example customers, suppliers, shareholders, the local community, government and financial providers.

Different stakeholders engage with businesses in a range of different ways. Table 1.1.4 provides examples of how different stakeholders may interact with a business.

**Table 1.1.4** Examples of how different stakeholders may interact with a business

| Stakeholder | Engagement |
| --- | --- |
| **Owners (sole traders and partners)** | The owners of a business are interested in how their business is doing, for example how much profit or loss is being made each year. Owners are then able to decide how much money they want to take from the business in the form of drawings. |
| **Shareholders** | Shareholders in limited companies are interested in whether the business is likely to continue in the foreseeable future. They want to know that their share investment money is safe and how much money they may receive back in dividends. |
| **Prospective owners** | Any person entering into an established business will want to know the financial viability of the business, the price of the ownership, the share price, etc. |
| **Management** | Managers require up-to-date information so that they can plan for the long-term future of the business. |
| **Government** | Businesses have to declare their financial records to determine their liability for taxation. In addition, government departments check compliance with various types of legislation, for example Health and Safety, Food Safety. |
| **Employees/ workers** | Employees and workers need to be assured of the future outlook and job security of their employment. They are interested in the working conditions at the business. |
| **Customers** | Customers need to be certain that a business organisation is going to sell them quality products at a price that they perceive to be 'value for money'. |
| **Suppliers** | Suppliers will need to ensure that the business organisation that they sell to will be able to pay for the goods they supply. In addition, the supplier would like to be assured that the business organisation will purchase from them in the future. |
| **Local community** | In many cases, the local community will provide the employees of the business organisation. The local community will also be concerned about pollution, for example late-night noise or smoke pollution. |
| **Finance providers** | Finance providers, for example a bank, need to ensure that any loans can be repaid on time and in full. |

**Figure 1.1.7** A business's stakeholders

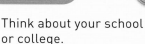

**Activity**

Think about your school or college.

● Make a list of all of the internal and external stakeholders for your school or college.

● In pairs, compare your lists and then prepare a table of how each of these stakeholders engages with the school or college.

## 1.4.3 Stakeholder engagement

Different stakeholders have different interests and engage with businesses in different ways. For example, some stakeholders have a financial interest in a business:

● **Owners/investors** have invested their own money in the business.

● **Shareholders** desire high annual dividends and would like the company share price to rise.

● **Managers** make decisions that influence financial performance.

● **Employees** are concerned about their jobs and would like a pay rise.

● **Banks** have lent, or plan to lend, money to the business.

By engaging with these stakeholder groups, organisations aim to benefit from their skills and abilities. For example:

● Ensuring the workforce is fully involved in the life of the business ensures that staff are highly motivated and operate to their full potential. It is also likely that the staff will remain at the business and not leave for other jobs. This will increase the retention rate of employees.

● Through engaging with customers, employees, residents, consumer groups, charities, etc., a business can build a good reputation in the local area. This provides the organisation with the opportunity to increase its sales and ultimately its profit levels.

● Fully engaged workers and managers are likely to have new and innovative ideas that can be used to further the success of the business.

- A business that fully engages with all of its stakeholders is likely to attract investors. This will mean that demand for shares in limited companies increases. An increase in demand will mean that the price of each share increases.

## Remember

- Stakeholders are any individuals who have an interest in a business.
- Internal stakeholders are those within the organisation.
- External stakeholders are those from outside of the organisation.
- Different stakeholders have different interests and engage with organisations in different ways.
- Businesses that engage with their stakeholders are likely to have increased staff motivation and retention, a good reputation, new ideas and an increased share price.

## Test yourself

1 Write a definition of stakeholder.
2 Explain the difference between internal and external stakeholders.
3 List the stakeholders of your school or college.

## Read about it

Branson, R. *Screw It, Let's Do It* (Virgin, 2006) – Provides practical business examples and details the lessons Richard Branson has learnt by running his businesses.

Jones, P. *Tycoon* (Hodder & Stoughton, 2007) – Provides entrepreneurial examples and explains how business dreams can be turned into reality.

Mawson, A. *The Social Entrepreneur: Making Communities Work* (Atlantic Books, 2008) – Considers the importance of social issues in making organisations successful.

**www.gov.uk/browse/business** – This website has useful information about different business operations.

**www.socialenterprise.org.uk** – Website of a national body for social enterprise; provides excellent practical examples.

# Learning outcome 2: Understand the marketing mix, market research, market types and orientation types

## 2.1 Marketing mix

The marketing mix is the different factors that can be controlled by a business in an attempt to influence customers to purchase its products. When a business markets its materials, it is important to consider the marketing mix (also known as the 4 Ps) shown in Figure 1.2.1.

| | |
|---|---|
| **Product**<br>how the product or service is designed or invented to make it something that customers will want to buy | **Price**<br>how the product or service is priced to make a profit |
| **Place**<br>how the product or service is distributed to customers | **Promotion**<br>how customers are informed about the product or service and persuaded to buy |

**Figure 1.2.1** The 4 Ps of the marketing mix – Product, Price, Place, Promotion

When marketing a product or service, a business aims to integrate all four aspects of the marketing mix to create a suitable brand image. No one element is more important than any other; they all link together. For example, a very poor product is unlikely to sell even if it is priced at a very low price. A business needs to ensure that products are appropriately priced, promoted and placed in the market.

**Figure 1.2.2** The marketing mix

## 2.1.1 Product types

Businesses categorise their products:

- Some products will be tangible – these are physical items that exist in the real world, for example a cup of coffee, a car, a mobile telephone, a teddy bear, etc.
- Other products are intangible – these are products or services that have no physical being, for example mobile phone networks, broadband, car insurance, etc.

In order for a business to be successful, it must differentiate its products from those of its rivals. This means it needs to make its products or services stand out from others that are available.

### Any product or service needs to establish a strong brand image

One way to make products or services stand out is to establish a strong brand image. Many businesses, for example McDonald's, have a very strong brand image.

#### Advantages
- The name of the business sells the goods or services without needing to do anything else to make them different.

#### Disadvantages
- The costs of developing a strong brand image can be extremely high. This may reduce profits if the strategy is unsuccessful.
- Developing a strong brand image takes a very long time. This is not a short-term strategy for a business.

### Identifying a clear unique selling point

Some businesses develop a **unique selling point (USP)**. This is a feature that separates a product from its competitors. There are a number of examples of products with identifiable USPs in the market today, for example:

- car performance, e.g. BMW, Porsche
- branding, e.g. Nike
- design, e.g. Apple.

#### Advantages
- The name of the business sells the goods or services without needing to do anything else to make them different.

#### Disadvantages
- The costs of developing clear USP can be extremely high. Once established, though, the USP should repay these costs.
- As with developing a strong brand image, identifying a clear USP takes a very long time. This is not a short-term strategy for a business.

**Key word**

**Unique selling point (USP)**: The key product feature that separates a product from its competitors.

**Figure 1.2.3** A product with an identifiable USP

## Design mix model

A number of businesses use a design mix model. Figure 1.2.4 shows a traditional product design mix.

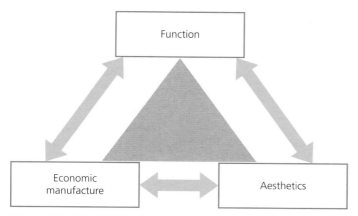

**Figure 1.2.4** A traditional product design mix

- **Function:** Any product must be able to perform the job for which it was designed.
- **Economic manufacture:** A product must be financially viable and cost-effective to produce. Materials appropriate to the product must be used, while also ensuring appropriate manufacturing costs.
- **Aesthetics:** How a product looks or feels is very important when trying to sell goods or services. For example, luxury cars often have a leather interior to create a luxurious feel.

Different businesses focus on different elements of the design mix, depending on the type of product and the type of customer it is aimed at. For example, in Figure 1.2.5 a washing machine manufacturer would focus on the function element of the design mix model (1 in the diagram), where as a luxury handbag design company would focus on the aesthetics of the bags it is designing (2 in the diagram).

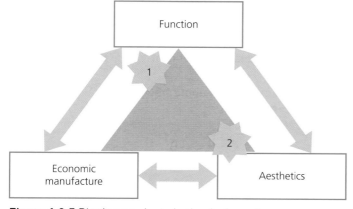

**Figure 1.2.5** Placing products in the design mix

**Activity**

Copy the design mix model in Figure 1.2.4. Place the following products where you think they belong in the design mix. Compare your decisions with those of a partner.

- Rolls-Royce car
- McDonald's Happy Meal
- Apple iPhone
- Computer desk
- Gold watch
- Supermarket value chicken
- Underground train

## Case study

Financial charities are keen to encourage young children to learn about money and how to save.

As part of their work with primary schools, one charity has decided to give out free money boxes to all the school's five-year-old children.

Answer the following question:

Using the appropriate features of the design mix model, create a design for a money box that the charity could use.

## Activity

In small groups, consider the technology industry and select a product to consider, for example a games console, computer or mobile phone.

● Discuss how your chosen product is differentiated from its competitors.
● In your discussion, consider brand image, USP and design mix model.
● Consider the advantages and disadvantages of each of the different ways used to differentiate the product.
● Each member of the group needs to think about how the product would meet their own particular needs.

## 2.1.2 Product lifecycle

All products have a unique **product lifecycle**. There are five main stages that generally occur, shown in Figure 1.2.6.

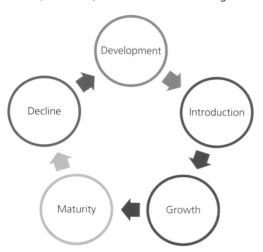

**Figure 1.2.6** The stages of the product lifecycle

**Key word**

**Product lifecycle**: Traces the journey of a product from its development and launch to its removal from sale to the public.

The lifecycle shows the stages a product goes through from its development and launch until it is removed from sale to the public. Some products naturally decline in popularity, while some never succeed; a few will continue to grow and survive in the market for many years.

**Table 1.2.1** The stages of the product lifecycle

| Lifecycle stage | Description |
| --- | --- |
| **Development** | During this stage, a business researches and develops the product before it is made available for sale to the customer. Product testing and trials take place. |
| **Introduction** | This is when a business launches the new product on the open market and makes it available for sale. The business advertises the product heavily during this stage in order to improve customer knowledge of the product and encourage sales. At this stage the company will be making low profits and possibly losing money and will have a low **market share**. |
| **Growth** | During this stage of the lifecycle, customers are familiar with the product and sales are increasing. At this time, the number of sales increases at its fastest rate and profits rise. Competitors may enter the market if the product is a success. |
| **Maturity** | During this stage, sales of the product have reached their highest. It is likely that the number of new customers is reducing and growth is limited. Other businesses may have entered the market to compete or the number of products available may mean the market is saturated. |
| **Decline** | In the decline phase, sales of the product begin to fall. Customers are no longer interested in the product and may have switched to newer alternative products. The business does not actively advertise the product and eventually removes it from sale. |

**Key word**

**Market share**: The section of a market controlled by a particular business.

A product lifecycle is usually represented on a graph like the one in Figure 1.2.7.

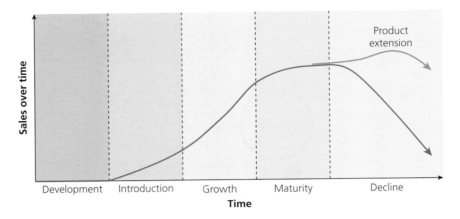

**Figure 1.2.7** The product lifecycle

## Activity

Label the product lifecycle diagram.

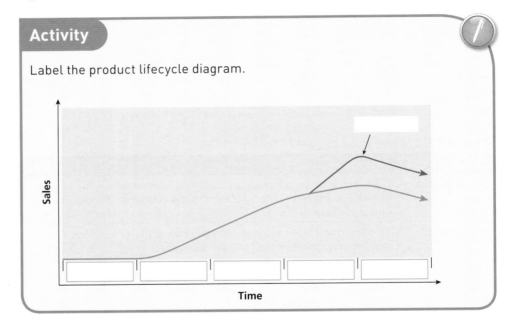

## Stretch activity

Identify the stages of a product lifecycle for a mobile phone.

In pairs, discuss how long each of the different stages may be and when the manufacturer is likely to introduce a new model.

## Product lifecycle-extension strategies

It is often cheaper for a business to make changes to a current product than to develop a brand-new product for sale. With this in mind, businesses do all they can to extend the life (the growth and maturity phases) of successful products.

There are a number of different **extension strategies** they can use to extend the life of a product:

### New advertising campaigns or new packaging

Businesses may devise new television advertisements in order to 'reintroduce' their products to the general public. The aim of an advertising campaign is to attract both new and existing customers.

New packaging is often a relatively cheap method of updating a product. Businesses brighten up their current packaging by changing the colours or logos, etc., in order to encourage customers to continue to purchase their product.

If a business provides improved packaging, customers may perceive an increase in quality and therefore be prepared to pay a higher price. Newly designed packaging may attract new customers and increase the number of sales. Packaging design can be expensive, though, and depending on the type of product or service may have a short life. For example, packaging introduced to coincide with a new film launch can be used for only a relatively short period of time.

### New pricing strategies

A business may reduce the selling price of its products and services to give an increased sense of perceived value. In contrast, increasing the selling price can increase revenue and profitability.

A business may decide to increase the price of its product or to reduce it. Increasing the price of a product makes more revenue and therefore more profit for a business. Raising the price of a product alongside a re-branding of the product may allow a business to enter the 'luxury' market. In this market, people are prepared to pay more for products, therefore increasing profit by selling the same volume of goods for a higher price.

Lowering the price of a product often makes it more attractive to both new and existing customers. Reducing the price of a product too much, however, can 'devalue' the product and make it seem 'worthless'. This might mean customers would be unwilling to purchase the product.

The disadvantages of increasing the product price are that it may mean customers buy their products from another retailer, if they feel that the increased price is not in line with other competitors. An increase in product price is also likely to mean that customers expect a better quality product. If this is not the case, a business may see a reduction in sales. If a business cuts the price of an existing product, this will reduce the amount of profit the organisation makes per unit. The business would therefore need to sell extra products in order to cover the loss in revenue.

### New product features

Different businesses add extra features and functions to their products and stores. For example, a number of fast-food restaurants offer drive-through facilities, table service and/or the option to order on screen. Depending on what is required, some changes to location, features and functions may be expensive to implement and so would reduce profits.

**Key word**

**Extension strategies**: Actions a business can take to extend the life of a product and increase sales.

**Figure 1.2.8** A product with added value: the Dyson V8 cordless vacuum cleaner

Adding value is a popular strategy which involves the business adding new features to an existing product. For example, adding extra memory to a mobile phone or creating a cordless version of a vacuum cleaner. This strategy works well for brands that are well known and have been popular for many years. By adding value, businesses can charge customers more for their products. This leads to increased revenue and therefore profitability. A business can add value by making premium products to differentiate itself from its competitors, meaning it will attract new customers.

Re-launching an existing product can be costly, however, and require considerable financial investment in terms of research, piloting, trialling and then marketing the updated product. Adding value will not be successful if there is no demand for the original product. Therefore, before adding value, a business will often check that there is likely to still be demand for the product in the future.

## Product development and innovation

The advantages of product development and innovation include:

- **Remaining competitive:** New product development should allow a business to attract new customers. This means that it will remain competitive and be able to compete with its rivals in the market. Without new products, customers will move to other providers.
- **Entering new markets:** If a business is selling a product that has universal appeal but has yet to target a full range of customers, then it could investigate offering the product for sale in new areas. This could include introducing a children's range of an adult product or starting to sell in different areas of the country.
- **Increasing market share:** New products enable a business to diversify and enter new markets. This will mean that it has the opportunity to increase its market share.

In cases where a business needs to differentiate itself further, it may decide to make improvements to its current product offering. Changes it may consider making include:

- **The product's location:** This could be the location of a product in a particular store or the geographical location where a product is sold. For example, a supermarket may increase the number of its stores that have a café or a pharmacy
- **The product's features and functions:** This is the different features and functions that a product has. For example, a mobile phone may have a large screen, be lightweight and have 32GB of memory, etc.
- **The product's design and appearance:** Many stores have 'face lifts' to increase their appeal.

**Figure 1.2.9** H&M is an existing brand that has adapted to appeal to a broader target audience

If a business can successfully tap into a new market, it may see its sales – and therefore its profits – increase considerably. This strategy may not be suitable for every product, however. Certain products may only be popular in certain geographic locations – for example, kilts may be popular in Scotland but have a limited market in Wales.

## 2.1.3 Boston Matrix

The Boston Matrix is a way of analysing the product portfolio offered for sale by a business. Businesses categorise their products into one of four categories. If a business has only a few products in its range and these are all in the same category, it is important that it tries to extend its product range.

- **Stars:** These are products that have a high market share in a fast-growing market.
- **Question marks:** These are products that have a low market share in a fast-growing market. These will be a cause for concern for the business owners and may need to be retired. They can be referred to as problem children.
- **Cash cows:** These are products that have a high market share in a slow-growing market. They tend to be highly successful products that stay in the market for many years.
- **Dogs:** These are products that have a low market share in a slow-growing market. Business owners will often remove these products from the market, unless they are needed to ensure sales of another, more successful product.

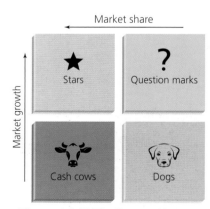

Figure 1.2.10 The Boston Matrix

## 2.1.4 Place

Place is the location where a business's products are made available to its customers. When making decisions about where to sell, a business needs to assess the cost effectiveness of each of the different ways that products can reach its customers.

### Factors affecting place

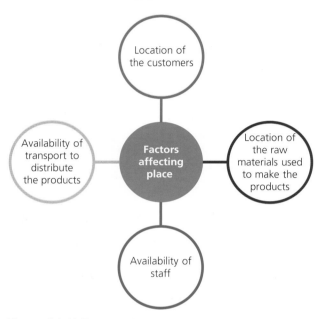

**Figure 1.2.11** Factors affecting place

### Channels of distribution

Potential channels of distribution include:

- **Retailers:** Goods and products are placed into shops so that customers can buy the products. The downside to this is that unless the shop is owned by the producer, profit levels will be lower as the producer will need to pay the retailer to sell its goods.

- **Wholesalers:** Some producers sell their goods using a wholesaler. These companies buy in bulk and then resell smaller quantities of goods to retailers. The downside to this is that unless the wholesaler is owned by the producer, profit levels will be lower as the producer will need to pay the wholesaler to sell its goods.

- **Direct selling:** Examples include mail order or telesales. The producer sells its products to customers without the need for a high street store. Producers often place their products in catalogues or on television.

- **Agents:** Some businesses employ agents to sell their products for them. In this case, an agent contacts potential customers and takes orders on behalf of the business. The agent is usually paid commission by the business, based on the number of sales they make.

## E-commerce

E-commerce is a low-cost method of marketing and selling goods. Producers often place their goods on their own website and sell direct to their customers. For customers, e-commerce provides a quick and easy way to purchase goods. There is a risk, however, that the products may not be as they look online, and many consumers are concerned about providing bank or card details online to complete purchases.

## 2.1.5 Price

Businesses make informed decisions about how to price a product based on their market research.

### Demand, supply and equilibrium price

The price of goods and services in a free market economy is determined by the interaction of demand and supply.

#### Demand

Demand is the amount of a product that consumers want. Changes in price will affect demand, as shown in Table 1.2.2.

There are several other factors that also affect the demand for a product:

- **Income:** If the incomes of the buyers of a product increase, it is likely that demand for the product will also increase.
- **The price of substitute goods:** For example, if the price of CDs increases, the demand for online downloads of digital music will also increase.
- **The price of complementary products:** For example, an increase in the price of cars will cause a decrease in the demand for petrol.
- **Changes in tastes and fashions:** For example, the decrease in demand for red meat in recent years.
- **Changes in the population:** For example, an ageing population will have an impact on the demand for winter sun holidays.
- **Advertising:** A successful advertising campaign will increase the demand for a product.
- **Legislation:** Changes to the law will affect demand for certain products, e.g. hands-free mobile phone kits.

#### Supply

Supply is the amount of a product that suppliers are willing to offer to the market at a given time. For example, a change in price will affect supply, as shown in Table 1.2.3.

Other factors that might cause a change in the level of supply include:

- **Cost of production:** For example, a fall in cost due to new technology.
- **The weather:** This can affect the amount of agricultural produce available for sale.
- **Taxation:** If firms are taxed highly on a certain product, they will offer less for sale.

**Activity**

Make a list of products that are sold via each of the following channels of distribution:

- retailers
- wholesalers
- mail order
- telesales
- internet selling.

**Table 1.2.2** The effect on demand of changes in price

| Price (£) | Demand |
|-----------|--------|
| 3 | 10 |
| 2 | 20 |
| 1 | 30 |

**Table 1.2.3** The effect on quantity supplied of changes in price

| Price (£) | Quantity supplied |
|-----------|-------------------|
| 3 | 30 |
| 2 | 20 |
| 1 | 10 |

### Equilibrium price

The price at which the demand and supply curves intersect is known as the equilibrium price. This is the price that a business should charge for its product.

## Cost plus pricing

In general terms, a business prices its product by working out what it costs to buy or make the product and then adding the amount of profit it would like to make. There is little point in selling a product for a lower price than it has cost to produce – the business would make a loss. A business needs to review other considerations as well, however, which are detailed below.

**Figure 1.2.12** Calculation of selling price

### Income level of target customers

The income level of a business's target customers must be taken into account. For example, luxury car dealers can charge high prices, as their customers earn high salaries. Budget supermarkets must charge low prices, as the majority of their customers earn low salaries.

### Price of competitor products

If a competitor is already selling a similar product, it would be difficult to sell a product for a price that is higher than that of the competitor, because customers would tend to choose the cheaper option.

If a business needs to lower the price of its products in order to compete, this will have a significant impact on its profit margin. Lowering prices is likely to lower its profit margins.

A bigger business will have more bargaining power and therefore can usually achieve lower production costs. In business terms, this is known as economies of scale. This means that larger businesses are able to sell at a more competitive (lower) price than smaller businesses.

It is important to remember that lowering the cost of any product always needs to be done with production cost and overall profits in mind.

### Types of pricing strategies and the appropriateness of each

A business can adopt various pricing strategies when selling to customers, as shown in Table 1.2.4.

**Table 1.2.4** Pricing strategies

| Pricing strategy | Target market | Pricing tactic | Advantages | Disadvantages |
|---|---|---|---|---|
| Competitive pricing | New and existing customers | The business sets a price that is similar to that of a local competitor. For example, supermarkets price matching goods. | May attract new customers as the price is the same as their usual retailer. | There is no price competition as all businesses are charging the same price, which could damage the business's ability to compete.<br><br>Profit margins are likely to be low as the selling price may only be sufficient to cover the production costs of the goods.<br><br>Businesses need to be creative in their methods of attracting customers, as the price alone will not encourage customers to the store. |
| Loss leaders | New and existing customers | The business is willing to make a loss on a product in order to get customers to purchase the product. It then increases the price once the customers like the product. | Attracts customers as it is perceived as a good deal. This may increase customer numbers, revenue and profit margins.<br><br>Products are sold for only a very small amount less than was originally planned. | Difficult to ensure customers will continue to purchase the products once the selling price increases. |
| Promotional pricing | New and existing customers | The business temporarily reduces the price of a product to increase interest in it. | Attracts customers to a particular product and attempts to make them purchase it.<br><br>Effective in quickly increasing market share. | Revenue is lost while selling at the lower cost, therefore profit margins are lower.<br><br>Products that have a very short lifespan, for example fashion clothing, are not suited to this method of pricing. By the time the price rises, the product is no longer in fashion. |
| Price skimming | New customers | The business introduces the product at a high price and then gradually lowers it over time. For example, when Dyson introduced its bagless cleaner there was no competitor, so it could charge very high prices. | High prices can give a product a good image.<br><br>A good image can lead customers to think the product is of very high quality.<br><br>Gives businesses high profits while the price is high. This additional money helps pay back research costs that have been incurred. | Some customers will be lost due to the high price.<br><br>Sales can be lost as customers are put off by the higher price, which reduces revenue.<br><br>There is a possibility that competitors will bring out lower-priced products and therefore sales will be lost. |
| Psychological pricing | New and existing customers | The business sets a price that appears to be attractive to a customer. For example, selling a holiday for £999 rather than £1000. | Attracts customers as it is perceived as a good deal. This may increase customer numbers, revenue and profit margins. | Difficult for cashiers to calculate the total amount owed.<br><br>Difficult to offer percentage discounts – for example, it is difficult to offer 10% off 99p. |

| Pricing strategy | Target market | Pricing tactic | Advantages | Disadvantages |
|---|---|---|---|---|
| Price penetration | New customers | The business introduces the product at a lower price than usual to attract customers. It then gradually increases the price over time. For example, selling a new flavour of crisps at half the price they will be sold at eventually. | Attracts customers to a particular product and attempts to make them purchase it. Price penetration is effective in quickly increasing market share. | Revenue is lost while selling at the lower cost, therefore profit margins are lower. Products that have a very short lifespan, for example fashion clothing, are not suited to this method of pricing. By the time the price rises, the product is no longer in fashion. |

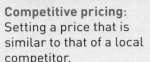

## Key words

**Competitive pricing:** Setting a price that is similar to that of a local competitor.

**Loss leaders:** A pricing tactic in which a business is willing to make a loss on a particular product in order to get customers to purchase the product.

**Price skimming:** Introducing a product at a high price, then gradually lowering the price over time.

**Psychological pricing:** Setting a price that appears attractive to a customer.

**Price penetration:** Introducing a product at a lower price than usual to attract customers, then gradually increasing the price over time.

**Promotional pricing:** A business tactic in which the price of a product is reduced in order to attract the attention of customers

**Burnley FC** @BurnleyOfficial · Apr 4

SALE | There are currently MASSIVE discounts at the Clarets Store with all replica shirts now £15, training tee's from just £10 and polo tops discounted to £12.50.

Visit the Clarets Store at Turf Moor, or go online at claretsstore.com to shop now!

**Figure 1.2.13** The use of pricing strategies

## 2.1.6 Promotion

### Advertising

Businesses may produce advertisements for their products. A wide range of advertising methods is available. These include:

- leaflets
- social media and websites
- newspapers
- magazines
- radio.

A business needs to ensure that its adverts focus on the target audience and the products that it is trying to sell.

### Advantages

- A successful advertising campaign can be an effective way of attracting new customers, as well as reminding existing customers how good a product is.
- Effective advertising has a wide coverage, meaning that a lot of different people will see the advertisements.
- Businesses have full control of their advertisements, meaning they can make sure the message they send out is the one that they wish to portray.
- As advertisements are often repeated regularly, the business's message can be effectively communicated and is likely to build brand loyalty.

### Disadvantages

- Advertising costs can be incredibly high.
- There is no guarantee that an advertising campaign will increase sales of the product, so it can be a financially risky strategy.
- Advertisements are impersonal, as they are aimed at a wide range of people.
- Advertisements are one-way communication and lack flexibility. They cannot be adjusted and do not allow customers to ask questions.

## Leaflets

Leaflets tend to be used by small businesses, as they are low-cost and can be targeted to customers in the local area. For example, fast-food takeaway shops often use leaflets to promote their menus.

### Advantages

- Leaflets are relatively cheap to produce and can contain a large amount of information.
- They can be targeted to customers in the local area.
- They can be distributed to a wide range of potential customers.
- They are easy to read and have a good visual impact.

### Disadvantages

- Leaflets are often thrown away once read if they are of poor quality.
- They can be seen as junk mail and not read.
- As leaflets are not usually kept for a long period of time, they do not have a long-term impact.

**Activity**

Fresh Food is a small supermarket based on the west coast of England. It is introducing a new range of salads.

- Analyse the advantages and disadvantages of the different pricing strategies that Fresh Food could use when introducing its new range of salads.
- Recommend which pricing strategy Fresh Food should use when launching the new range of salads.

## Social media and websites

The use of websites to advertise products is a rapidly growing area for many businesses. Businesses can choose to:

- place adverts on search engine results pages
- pay for pop-ups (these are small internet windows that appear over the top of web pages and are used to attract attention)
- place adverts on social networking sites.

A number of businesses also have their own websites and social media accounts, for example on Facebook or Twitter.

### Advantages

- Adverts on social media and websites are relatively cheap to produce and distribute.
- Websites and social media accounts can be used to update customers on current offers, new products and promotions.
- Adverts on social media and websites have been proved to increase sales.
- Social media and websites allow access to international markets.
- Social media accounts and websites allow customers to provide feedback.

### Disadvantages

- Adverts on social media and websites are less useful if targeting an older market who are less 'tech savvy' and less likely to go online or use apps.
- Social media requires daily monitoring to prevent inappropriate behaviour.
- There are risks of negative reviews, information leaks or hacking.

**Figure 1.2.14** Advertising on a social media account

## Newspapers

It is estimated that about one-quarter of all expenditure on advertising in the UK is on newspaper adverts.

Businesses need to decide whether they want to advertise in national newspapers, local newspapers or free newspapers. Free and local newspaper advertisements are relatively cheap, whereas large adverts in national newspapers are extremely expensive. Small businesses tend to focus on free and local newspapers to keep costs down and to target the customers who are likely to purchase their products.

### Advantages

- The costs of advertising in free and local newspapers are low.
- Local newspaper advertising can target local customers, directing them to specific local outlets.
- National newspapers are more widely read than local newspapers.
- National newspapers have a broader reach.
- Newspaper advertising is effective in targeting the older generation, who often read newspapers on a daily basis.

### Disadvantages

- Advertising in national newspapers is very expensive.
- Unless the advert is in a prime position, there may be competition for the reader's attention.
- Newspaper adverts are not targeted.
- Newspaper adverts are less effective when targeting the younger generation.

**Figure 1.2.15** Advertising in a newspaper

## Magazines

Magazines are usually issued on a weekly or monthly basis and focus their articles on a specific target market of readers. While magazine advertisements are generally more expensive than those in a newspaper, it is likely that the information will reach the specific customers the business is trying to target. It is also important to remember that individuals tend to keep magazines for longer than newspapers.

### Advantages

- Advertisements in magazines are targeted. Magazines target specific groups and therefore advertisements can be placed accordingly.
- Unlike leaflets, people tend to keep magazines.
- People often pass magazines they have purchased and read on to their family or friends so the adverts may reach a wider audience.

### Disadvantages

- Deadlines for magazine advertisements may be months in advance. Good business planning is therefore required to know the advertising that will be needed several months in advance.
- Depending on the type of magazine chosen, costs can be very high.
- Magazines contain a vast amount of advertisements. There is a risk that the business's advertisement will be lost among them.

## Radio

Businesses tend to use specific radio stations for their particular target market. For example, a sportswear store may use a football show on its local radio station to advertise its new range of football shirts.

### Advantages

- Use of sounds and music can make radio advertisements attract attention.
- Specific audiences can be targeted by choosing an appropriate station and programme on which to advertise.
- Radio advertisements can be produced very quickly.
- Radio advertisements are considerably cheaper than advertising on television.

### Disadvantages

- Radios are often used as background noise, so advertisements can be missed or ignored.
- Prime slots in the morning or evening when people are driving to and from work are considerably more expensive than other times during the day.
- There is no way to save an advertisement, so the listener needs to take in all of the information at once.

### Activity

Claret Gym, in Turf Town, has been open for two months. The gym is independently owned and is not part of a national chain. There are several other larger gyms in the town but the customer service at Claret Gym is its unique selling point when attracting customers.

Complete a table like the one below to advise the owners on the most appropriate advertising methods to attract and retain members.

| Advertising method | Description | Advantages | Disadvantages |
|---|---|---|---|
|  |  |  |  |
|  |  |  |  |
|  |  |  |  |

## Sales promotion

Sales promotions are used by businesses to provide a short-term boost to their sales. A number of different techniques can be used, shown in Figure 1.2.16.

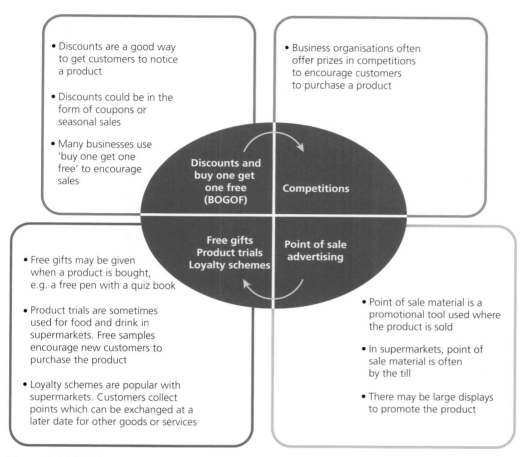

- Discounts are a good way to get customers to notice a product
- Discounts could be in the form of coupons or seasonal sales
- Many businesses use 'buy one get one free' to encourage sales

- Business organisations often offer prizes in competitions to encourage customers to purchase a product

**Discounts and buy one get one free (BOGOF)**

**Competitions**

**Free gifts Product trials Loyalty schemes**

**Point of sale advertising**

- Free gifts may be given when a product is bought, e.g. a free pen with a quiz book
- Product trials are sometimes used for food and drink in supermarkets. Free samples encourage new customers to purchase the product
- Loyalty schemes are popular with supermarkets. Customers collect points which can be exchanged at a later date for other goods or services

- Point of sale material is a promotional tool used where the product is sold
- In supermarkets, point of sale material is often by the till
- There may be large displays to promote the product

**Figure 1.2.16** Different kinds of sales promotion

Businesses always have key objectives when completing any promotional activity. These include:

- increasing consumer knowledge
- increasing market share
- communicating with customers
- encouraging purchasing
- developing customer loyalty.

## Personal selling

Personal selling is when a salesperson sells a product to a client after meeting them face to face. The skills of the salesperson often determine the quantity of goods or services that are sold. Personal selling is often used in the finance industry to sell investments or pensions.

**Figure 1.2.17** A sales display in a shop window

## Direct marketing

Direct marketing is when businesses sell products or services directly to the public. They may use mail order, online or telephone sales rather than selling via another retailer.

Claret Gym, in Turf Town, has been open for two months. The gym is independently owned and is not part of a national chain. There are several other larger gyms in the town but the customer service at Claret Gym is its unique selling point when attracting customers.

Complete a table like the one below to advise the owners of Claret Gym on the most appropriate sales promotion techniques it could use to attract and retain members.

| Sales promotion technique | Description | Advantages | Disadvantages |
|---|---|---|---|
|  |  |  |  |
|  |  |  |  |
|  |  |  |  |

**Activity**

Carry out research online to review the loyalty schemes available at three different supermarkets.

- Prepare a table that compares and contrasts the features of each loyalty scheme.
- Write a paragraph to explain which supermarket's loyalty scheme most attracts you as a customer.

**Remember**

- The marketing mix is the different factors that can be controlled by a business in an attempt to influence customers to purchase its products.
- The marketing mix is known as the 4 Ps – Product, Price, Place, Promotion.
- The design mix model considers the link between function, economic manufacture and aesthetics.
- There are five key parts to a product lifecycle – development, introduction, growth, maturity and decline.
- An extension strategy is used to extend the life of an existing product.
- The Boston Matrix is a way of analysing the product portfolio offered for sale by a business.
- The Boston Matrix divides an organisation's products into Stars, Question marks, Cash cows and Dogs.

**Test yourself**

1 Write a definition of unique selling point. Provide an example to illustrate your answer.
2 Explain how a business may use the design mix model.
3 Identify **and** describe the main sections of the product lifecycle.
4 Explain **two** extension strategies that could be used to extend the life of a product.
5 Explain how the selling price of a product is decided.
6 Write a definition of competitor pricing.
7 Identify **and** describe **three** advertising methods that could be used by a clothing retailer.
8 Identify **and** describe **three** sales promotion techniques.

## 2.2 Market research and markets

**Market research** involves finding out information about the market in which the business operates and is a vital part of any business success. Market research is used throughout a business's life. It is vital to research the potential market when setting up a business, but market research cannot stop at this stage. Customers and the market as a whole change over time, therefore it is very important to complete in-depth market research on a regular basis. This may be to assess whether new products should be introduced, existing products should be phased out, expansion plans should take place, or in certain circumstances whether there is a long-term future for the business.

**Key word**

**Market research**: The actions of a business to gather information about customers' needs and wants.

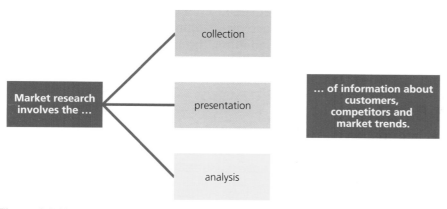

**Figure 1.2.18** Market research

In small businesses, such as sole traders, the owner often completes the market research. In large companies, specialist staff are employed in marketing departments to complete specialised market research to meet the needs of the organisation. Other businesses may work with marketing companies or agencies, which complete the market research on their behalf.

Businesses aim to find out what existing and potential customers need and would like to buy. They complete market research for the following reasons:

- **To understand the market and to reduce risk:** Comprehensive market research allows a business to understand the needs of the market so that it can provide the goods and services to meet those needs. By developing a working knowledge of customer needs and wants, the business reduces the risk of making inaccurate decisions about products or services. Although this is a major benefit to an organisation, many businesses opt out of completing market research due to the costs involved. These businesses often try to guess what customers may want to purchase. Alternatively, organisations may just contact existing customers to try to identify changes in taste and other market trends.

- **To gain customers' views and understand their needs, and to aid decision-making:** By understanding customer needs and wants, managers can make informed decisions. Market research allows customers to discuss their views, needs and wants in terms of products and services offered. Once analysed, this information provides a business with a comprehensive overview of what needs to be produced and sold in order to meet its customers' expectations. By meeting these expectations, the business is likely to maximise its sales and profits.

- **To inform product development and to promote the organisation:** Comprehensive and accurate market research reduces the risk when launching new or updated products. Whenever a business launches a new product, there is a possibility that customers will not want to buy it. By completing appropriate research, the business can reduce this risk, as it will be aware of what customers are looking to purchase in the future. Analysed market research information ensures the products that are developed are up-to-date and meet the needs of the business's customers. In addition, the business is promoting itself when asking customers about their needs, which may lead to additional sales from these customers.

## 2.2.1 Data types

Factual information that is collected, for example information about customers' ages, is known as **quantitative data**. Information about people's opinions and views is known as **qualitative data**.

Quantitative data is useful for statistical analysis and review, whereas qualitative information provides a business with a much more in-depth understanding of key issues. Quantitative information provides numerical data and gives an overview, but it does not provide any information about the reasoning behind the data.

**Internal data** is data and information held by a business. When completing market research, any business must ensure it reviews all its internal information alongside any external information that is available.

Businesses hold a wide range of information, for example sales data, customer profiles and financial budgets. Any numerical data can be used to predict the future by looking for trends over a period of time. Numerical data can also be compared against local competitors or against industry benchmarks.

## 2.2.2 Primary research

**Primary research** (also known as field research) is the gathering of data and information that has not been collected before. Methods of primary research include questionnaires, observations, focus groups, telephone surveys and consumer trials.

## Surveys and questionnaires

Surveys and questionnaires are popular methods of collecting primary (field) research. In many cases, surveys are completed through questionnaires. It is important to remember that businesses must comply with data protection legislation (GDPR) when processing survey data.

### Personal surveys

Personal surveys are where individuals are asked questions face to face.

### Advantages

- The information that is gained is accurate and relevant.
- If clarification is required, the interviewer can explain the questions to the interviewee.
- Personal surveys can take place in the street, in the entrance to a store or in a pre-arranged meeting place.

### Disadvantages

- Personal surveys are expensive to complete and extremely time-consuming.

### Postal surveys

In postal surveys, a large number of questionnaires are printed and distributed to individuals at their home address. Prior to distribution, the business needs to decide what sample size should be used and to whom the questionnaires should be sent. To ensure understandability, the questions need to be well written and it must be clear how participants are expected to complete the questionnaire. In order to get responses, questions should be short and are often multiple choice.

### Advantages

- Postal surveys are cheaper than personal surveys.

### Disadvantages

- It is difficult to gain any detailed answers. Businesses need to understand that many people see postal surveys as 'junk mail' and do not respond. It is often assumed that 90 per cent of these surveys will not be returned.

**Figure 1.2.19** Conducting a face-to-face survey

### Internet surveys

Online surveys are increasingly popular. The questions must be easy to read and understand, as there is no personal contact to explain meanings.

**Figure 1.2.20** An internet survey

## Advantages

● Online surveys are quick to produce and analyse.

## Disadvantages

● As with telephone surveys, a high proportion will not be answered.

It needs to be remembered that, while the internet can be used to conduct primary research, it would not be categorised as a stand-alone research method. Instead it is 'digital tools' such as websites, apps and social media, etc. that are directly used to conduct the primary research.

### Telephone surveys

Many businesses use telephone surveys.

## Advantages

● Telephone surveys can cover a wide geographical area.

## Disadvantages

● Telephone surveys are relatively expensive, as they are time-consuming in terms of staff time.
● Many people fail to complete the surveys as they do not answer the telephone calls or hang up.

## Observations

Observations involve watching and noting down what individuals do and how they behave in a particular situation. Retail stores use them frequently, with the aim of providing the most effective and efficient store layout. Businesses have to assess whether it is worth the cost outlay of completing an observation for the information that is likely to be learned.

### Advantages

- If one aisle in a store had made very few sales for a month, an observation may identify whether customers were avoiding the aisle or just not purchasing its goods.

### Disadvantages

- While it is possible to identify what is happening, an observation does not provide the reason why.
- Completing any observation is time-consuming and therefore costly.

## Focus groups

**Focus groups** usually provide high quality research information. A small group of individuals is chosen based on the needs of the business. The individuals are usually a cross-section of the public, to ensure there is a wide range of views. The group then discusses key questions and themes that have been identified by the business.

### Advantages

- Focus groups provide high quality information.
- Responses are focused on the business.

### Disadvantages

- Focus groups are costly and time-consuming to set up.

> **Key word**
>
> **Focus group:** A group of people who participate in a discussion about products and services.

> **Case study**
>
> Professional football clubs are keen to provide access for all. In recent years, they have introduced focus groups to discuss with fans what their needs and wants are. Following such focus groups, the football clubs have introduced a wide range of initiatives to increase supporter enjoyment. These have included: fan zones that are open prior to games, family areas, match day mascot opportunities, etc.
>
> Answer the following question:
>
> In small groups, identify a local professional sports team. Discuss potential initiatives that could be discussed should a focus group be held with its fans.
>
>
>
> **Figure 1.2.21** Burnley FC's match day mascot, Bertie Bee

## Consumer trials

A consumer trial is a short-term offering with the intention of gaining market research information by allowing consumers to examine, use or test goods prior to the business fully launching any new product.

### Advantages

- Consumer trials provide honest and reliable information.

### Disadvantages

- Consumer trials are expensive to operate and the responses are often difficult to analyse.
- Analysis of individuals' views and opinions is not as easy as analysis of numerical data.

## 2.2.3 Secondary research

> **Key word**
>
> **Secondary (desk) research**: Gathering data and information that has already been collected.

**Secondary research** (also known as desk research) involves gathering data and information that has already been collected before. Methods of secondary research include government reports, news articles, competitors' data and research papers.

## Government reports

Government publications and statistics are readily available to download. Depending on the information required, there might be a cost. The information is accurate and trustworthy, but it may be out of date – for example, the census is completed only once every ten years. Any government information will be generic and not specific to the requirements and situation of the business that downloads the information.

## News articles

Newspapers and trade magazines can be in either digital or physical format. These are relatively cheap to acquire, accurate and readily available. Physical books, newspapers and trade magazines can either be purchased or borrowed from local libraries. The information may be out of date, however, and may not be totally relevant to the business.

## Competitors' data

Competitors' data may be available publicly, depending on the legal structure of the business. Any limited company has to publish its financial data on an annual basis. In the UK, this is submitted to Companies House and is publicly available. By reviewing the financial records of other organisations, managers can review their own business's performance. It must be remembered that for meaningful comparisons to be made, data should only be compared 'like with like'. This means that a limited company should not be compared with a sole trader.

## Research papers

A number of market research companies are willing to sell businesses research material. Before purchasing any research material, it is important that an organisation considers the quality of the material. It could consider:

- What will this purchased report tell me?
- Can I purchase only the part of the report that is relevant to me?
- Who is the author?
- When was the report written?
- Which report is best for me?

As with other secondary (desk) research, it must be remembered that the information could be out of date and not totally relevant to the particular circumstances being considered.

**Table 1.2.5** Summary of primary (field) and secondary (desk) research

| Type of market research | Definition | Examples | Advantages | Disadvantages |
|---|---|---|---|---|
| **Primary (field) research** | Gathering data and information that has not been collected before. | Interviews Observations Questionnaires Surveys Focus groups Consumer trials | Relevant and up-to-date information. The data and information are specific to the business completing the research. Only available to the organisation that has commissioned the research, giving it a competitive advantage. | Costly and time-consuming to complete. A sample size that is too small may provide biased results. Consumers are not always willing to take part in market research. They often see telephone calls to gain information as 'nuisance calls'. |
| **Secondary (desk) research** | Gathering data and information that has already been collected. | Books, trade magazines, newspapers Published company reports Internal data Competitors' data Government publications and statistics Purchased research material | Cheaper than primary (field) research and often free, as the data and information already exist. The information and data is frequently based on a large sample size, for example census data. The information and data is readily available, therefore its collection is not time-consuming for the business. | The information is available to all, therefore restricting the competitive advantage to be gained. The information and data is not specific to the business completing the analysis. Depending on when the information was collected, it could be out of date and therefore irrelevant in current market conditions. |

## Activity

Working in pairs, categorise the following as either primary (field) or secondary (desk) research methods.

- reports from the Office of National Statistics
- internet research
- the annual financial report of a local competitor
- national newspaper articles
- focus groups
- census reports
- observations
- questionnaires.

## Activity

A new fast food restaurant is opening in Northern Town. Copy and complete the following table to advise the owners on the most appropriate primary (field) and secondary (desk) research methods to gain market information.

| Research method | Description | Advantages | Disadvantages |
|---|---|---|---|
|  |  |  |  |
|  |  |  |  |
|  |  |  |  |
|  |  |  |  |
|  |  |  |  |
|  |  |  |  |

## 2.2.4 Market types

A market is a place where buyers and sellers come together to interact and exchange goods.

**Figure 1.2.22** A market is a place where buyers and sellers come together

## Mass markets

A mass market is one in which goods or services are produced in large quantities and are aimed at most of the market. ITV is an example of such a business. To operate in such a market, a business must be able to produce goods on a large scale. This requires high investment in equipment and recruitment of staff.

Mass markets generally have:

- a high number of sales
- a large number of competitors
- a wide customer base
- low profit margins.

The advantage of operating in a mass market is that businesses should be able to produce goods more cheaply and benefit from economies of scale.

## Niche markets

A niche market is one in which goods or services are produced in small quantities and are aimed at a particular, often tiny, segment of the market. It is the opposite of a mass market, where products and services are produced for whole markets.

Niche markets generally have:

- a small sales volume
- a small number of customers
- highly specialised products
- potentially high profit margins.

The advantages of operating in a niche market include:

- A small business may be able to survive because it is offering a product or service that a larger organisation would find uneconomical to supply. The existing competitors might react aggressively if a smaller business tries to compete in the mass market.
- The business may be able to operate on a small scale. Many niche markets are relatively small and specialised. Small businesses are able to meet demand in the market, whereas they might lack resources to meet demand in the mass market.

## 2.2.5 Orientation types

Businesses develop their new products based on one of two orientations: market orientated or product orientated.

- A **market-orientated** business produces goods based on customer wants and needs. It will undertake high levels of market research to find out what the customers' wants and needs are. These businesses tend to be most successful. Examples may include food and drink manufacturers.
- A **product-orientated** business produces only goods that it is good at making. It has low levels of engagement with its potential customers.

**Key words**

**Market-orientated business**: Produces goods based on customer wants and needs.

**Product-orientated business**: Produces only goods that it is good at making.

Although the business produces high quality goods, these may not meet customer needs and therefore not be easy to sell to customers.

## Test yourself

1. Write a definition of market research.
2. Identify **five** sources of primary (field) research.
3. Identify **five** types of market segmentation.
4. Explain the advantages of a business segmenting its customers.
5. Assess the benefits of an existing business conducting primary (field) **and** secondary (desk) research.

## Remember

- Market research is a vital part of any business success. It involves finding out information about the market in which the organisation operates.
- Internal data is numerical or other data and information that is held by a business.
- Primary research (also known as field research) is the gathering of data and information that has not been collected before. Methods of primary research include observations, surveys, focus groups and consumer trials.
- Secondary research (also known as desk research) involves the gathering of data and information that has already been collected. Methods of secondary research include books, news articles and competitors' data.
- Niche marketing involves a business aiming a product at a particular – often tiny – segment of a market.
- Mass marketing involves products being aimed at whole markets rather than particular parts of them.
- A market-orientated business produces goods based on customer wants and needs.
- A product-orientated business produces only goods that it is good at making.

## Read about it

Cave, S. *Consumer Behaviour in a Week* (Hodder & Stoughton, 2002) – Details fundamental principles of consumer behaviour.

Christopher, M., Payne, A. and Ballantyne, D. *Relationship Marketing: Creating Stakeholder Value* (Routledge, 2002) – Considers how a business can benefit from its stakeholders.

Dibb, S., Simkin, L., Pride, W.M. and Ferrell, O.C. *Marketing: Concepts and Strategies* (Houghton Mifflin, 2005) – Reviews the main marketing concepts and strategies used in business.

Gummersson, E. *Total Relationship Marketing: Rethinking Marketing Management, 2nd edition* (Butterworth-Heinemann, 2002) – Provides an introduction to total relationship marketing and is good background reading.

**www.gov.uk/browse/business** – This website has useful information about different business operations.

**www.socialenterprise.org.uk** – Website of a national body for social enterprise; provides excellent practical examples.

# Learning outcome 3: Understand operations management

## 3.1 Operations management

### 3.1.1 Outsourcing

When organisations grow, they are often not able to complete all of the business tasks themselves. They need to outsource some of their operations. This means the organisation hires another business to do some of the work for it, for example payroll operations, IT operations or website design.

Small businesses, for example sole traders, also outsource various aspects of their work as they do not have all of the necessary skills to do the work themselves.

The outsourced work is usually of high quality but is considerably more expensive than if it was completed in-house.

### 3.1.2 Lean production

Lean production is a management approach that aims to cut waste and at the same time focuses on high quality. The idea is used throughout a business, from design to distribution.

There are different methods of lean production. These include just-in-time production, cell production, kaizen, and also benchmarking (see page 57).

#### Just-in-time

Just-in-time (JIT) production means that stock arrives on the production line just as it is needed. This minimises the amount of stock that has to be stored, and so reduces storage costs.

JIT has many benefits and may appear an obvious way to organise production, but it is a complicated process that requires efficient handling.

**Table 1.3.1** Just-in-time production

| Advantages | Disadvantages |
|---|---|
| Improves cash flow as stock is not tied up in storage | Needs suppliers and employees to be reliable |
| Reduces waste – stock does not go out of date | May be difficult to manage if there are surges in demand |
| Requires less factory storage space | Potential for loss of reputation if orders are delivered late |

## Cell production

Cell production:

- divides the production process into a series of stages
- is arranged around teams
- ensures each team completes a full unit of production, instead of individuals completing one task
- allows each team to have responsibility for their work and to see end results
- increases motivation
- increases responsibility
- improves quality.

**Figure 1.3.1** Cell production

## Kaizen

Kaizen is a Japanese concept that focuses on gradual and continuous improvement. The idea is a whole-business philosophy, and to ensure its success it is important that everyone in the organisation buys into the concept and vision.

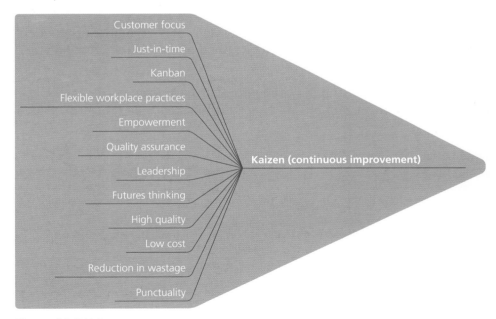

**Figure 1.3.2** Kaizen

## 3.1.3 Maintaining and improving quality
### Quality control

**Quality control** is an important aspect of any business. This is when an organisation checks that its products and services meet the required standards, so that customers will be satisfied when they purchase the product or service. For example, imagine if you purchased your favourite chocolate bar, and it did not taste the same as it normally does or it contained nuts when it didn't normally. These situations would demonstrate that the quality control processes at the manufacturer were not correct. It is important therefore that a business informs potential investors what it will be doing to ensure that its quality standards are high.

### Benchmarking

Benchmarking is the continuous, systematic search for and implementation of best practice that leads to superior performance. The use of benchmarking aids a business in maintaining and improving quality.

Businesses that benchmark measure their performance against that of others and aim to learn from the best firms in the world. Businesses use benchmarking to assess:

- the reliability of their products
- their ability to deliver items on time
- their ability to send out correct invoices
- the time taken to produce their products.

### Quality assurance

Most businesses have a quality assurance system where they maintain a certain level of quality for every product or service that they produce and sell. Usually this means that they focus on every stage of the production and delivery processes.

### Total Quality Management

Total Quality Management (TQM) is a management approach that seeks to involve all employees in the process of improving quality.

**Key word**

**Quality control:** When a business checks that its products and services meet the required standards, so that customers will be satisfied when they purchase them.

### 3.1.4 Production methods

Businesses tend to use one of the four different production methods shown in Table 1.3.2.

**Table 1.3.2** The four different production methods

| Production method | Description | Examples |
|---|---|---|
| **One-off production/ job production** | One product is made at a time. Every product will be slightly different and usually made by hand and/or machine. The products will be expensive and very time-consuming to make. | Paintings<br>Handmade jumpers<br>Bespoke jewellery |
| **Batch production** | Small quantities of identical products are made. This method uses machinery and manpower. The products tend to be relatively expensive due to the labour costs.<br>Each batch will be slightly different. | Coloured paint<br>Knitting wool |
| **Mass production** | This is usually completed on a production line and involves the assembly of different components or items.<br>It is usually completed by machine and relatively cheap to operate. | Cars<br>T-shirts<br>Motorised parts |
| **Continuous flow** | This is similar to mass production except that the production line is operated 24 hours a day, 7 days a week. This reduces the costs of stopping and starting production. Very few workers are required and the majority of the work is completed by machine. | Canned baked beans<br>Mass-produced loaves of bread |

**Figure 1.3.3** A continuous flow production line

### Activity

Working in pairs, write a list of businesses in your local area.

Decide which of the four different production methods is used by each of the businesses you identified.

## Remember

- Lean production is a management approach that aims to cut waste.
- Just-in-time (JIT) means that stock arrives on the production line just as it is needed. This minimises the amount of stock that has to be stored (reducing storage costs).
- Cell production divides production processes into a series of stages.
- Quality control occurs when a business checks that its products and services meet the required standards, so that its customers will be satisfied when they purchase the product or service.
- Benchmarking is the continuous, systematic search for and implementation of best practice, which leads to superior performance.
- Total Quality Management (TQM) is a management approach that tries to ensure all employees are involved in the process of improving quality.
- There are a number of different production methods. These include job production, batch production, mass production and continuous flow.

## Test yourself

1 Which type of production would be most appropriate for making canned soft drinks?
2 Write a definition of batch production.
3 Write a definition of lean production.
4 Explain how outsourcing is used by a business.
5 Explain why a business will use benchmark data.

## Read about it

Barrat, C. and Whitehead, M. *Buying for Business: Insights in purchasing and supply management* (Wiley, 2004) – Provides answers to key questions about purchasing and supply management in organisations.

Emmett, S. *Supply Chain in 90 Minutes* (Management Books, 2004) – Provides a concise practical introduction to supply chain management.

Green, J. *Starting Your Own Business* (How to Books, 2005) – Provides a step-by-step guide to how an entrepreneur should set up a business.

Hughes, V. and Weller, D. *Setting up a Small Business* (Hodder & Stoughton, 2006) – Provides guidance and advice on how an entrepreneur should set up a small business.

**www.gov.uk/browse/business** – This website has useful information about different business operations.

**www.socialenterprise.org.uk** – Website of a national body for social enterprise; provides excellent practical examples.

# Learning outcome 4: Understand internal influences on business

## 4.1 Customer service and internal influences and challenges of growth

### 4.1.1 Customer service

Customer service is the way in which a business looks after its customers. Excellent customer service ensures that a business attracts new customers and retains its existing ones.

Excellent customer service will:

- provide word-of-mouth promotion
- improve business reputation
- encourage repeat business
- set the business apart from its competitors
- provide brand awareness
- ensure customer loyalty and encourage customers to purchase from the business in the future.

In order to provide excellent customer service, employees will need:

- good communication skills for interacting with customers
- patience to understand customers' needs and wants
- attention to detail – it is important that employees focus on customer requirements
- good product knowledge
- excellent personal presentation skills – employees need to be appropriately dressed and act in a manner that will attract and retain customers.

Many businesses treat their staff as their most valuable asset. Employees who have excellent product knowledge and who are able to engage customers about the products and services are likely to attract and retain customers.

Businesses have learnt that it is not only important for their staff to engage with customers before and during a sale, they also need to offer excellent after-sales services too.

Businesses look to employ customer service assistants who are able to deal with exchanges and queries about deliveries and damaged products, or simply advise on how to use a product. Employees need to enjoy dealing with customers, be happy, friendly and helpful, not moody and rude, etc.

## Activity

In pairs, think about where you have experienced poor customer service.

- What made it bad, and how did it make you feel about that particular business?
- What would you expect to see from excellent customer service?

## Case study

Over the last 20 years, the cruise industry has grown in popularity. There is now a large number of franchised cruise specialists offering cruise holidays to passengers.

In order to differentiate themselves from other travel agents, these cruise specialists offer excellent customer service. They are usually experienced cruise passengers themselves, so they can offer excellent product information and are frequently available seven days a week to offer advice to passengers before they travel, during the cruise and on their return.

**Figure 1.4.1** The cruise industry

Answer the following question:

Identify **and** explain **three** factors that travel agents need to consider when using customer service to attract and retain customers.

## 4.1.2 Customer service measurements

When completing market research, a business needs to consider how it will receive feedback from its customers. In recent years, many organisations have started to send online surveys to their customers to review their experience. Hotels are keen to do this and often send guests forms to review their stay after leaving. Motor garages frequently telephone their customers to review the services offered during a visit to the dealership. Smaller businesses often have comment cards where customers can leave opinions and views about customer service.

By making customer service measurements, a business is able to:

- make informed decisions about its future product development – by having detailed information about what customers need and want, organisations can develop products to meet these needs
- **retain customers** – by meeting and responding to their customers' needs, businesses ensure that customers will return to them and purchase goods from them in the future
- remain competitive – by meeting customers' needs and listening to what customers think of its products and services, a business will be able to continue to make sales and therefore remain competitive in the market
- identify areas of strength and weakness by asking customers for their opinions, both positive and negative.

## 4.1.3 How customer service is measured

Businesses have to make a decision about how to measure customer service. They might use:

- repeat business data – the number of customers who return to the business to purchase their goods and services
- the number of complaints and compliments gathered over a period of time
- mystery shoppers, who enter a business to make a purchase and then review the performance of the organisation in terms of how they were treated and served
- social media/online communities with reviews and comments
- online surveys
- customer comment cards
- comments made to staff members
- telephone/email surveys
- email contact forms.

Customer feedback is very important to new businesses. Without a clear understanding of what customers need and want, a new business is unlikely to succeed. For example, an entrepreneur considering opening a new children's indoor play area would be likely to conduct primary and secondary research. They could:

- ask parents of young children to complete questionnaires
- conduct focus groups in local primary schools
- research online the number of other play areas in the local area
- research national statistics to find out the number of children in the target area
- visit competitor play areas, to ascertain what activities and facilities are currently being offered.

## Stretch activity

Analyse why it is important for a new business to identify and research its target market.

## Remember

- Customer service is the way in which a business looks after its customers.
- Excellent customer service ensures that a business attracts new customers and retains its existing ones.
- In order to provide excellent customer service, employees need certain attributes, for example good communication skills, patience, attention to detail.
- Customer feedback is very important to new businesses. Without having a clear understanding of what its customers need and want, a new organisation is unlikely to succeed.
- Businesses have to decide how to measure customer service.

## Test yourself

1 Write a definition of customer service.
2 List **five** attributes employees require to provide excellent customer service.
3 Describe the benefits a business gains from providing effective customer service.

# 4.2 Internal influences

There are four main **functional areas** that need to be considered when starting a new business, as shown in Figure 1.4.2.

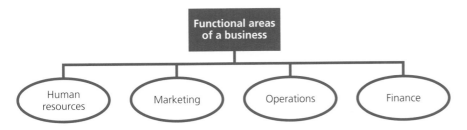

Figure 1.4.2 The four main functional areas

## Key word

**Functional area**: A department that plays a specific role within an organisation and whose employees carry out a particular aspect of the work of an organisation.

Small businesses, including many sole trader businesses, do not have different departments for each of these functions. They simply have one person who has to carry out all of these activities. Although this cuts costs and meets the business's needs, it is unlikely that the individual will be skilled in each of these areas. The individual may have a general overview of knowledge but lack a detailed understanding of the different areas.

## Aims and objectives

The aim of businesses is to target customers and ensure they are fully aware of what the organisation offers. Businesses therefore work to develop an understanding of the needs and wants of their customers and are responsible for promotional activities that help to generate sales and business growth.

**Figure 1.4.3** Marketing and promotional activities

## Financial position of the business and enterprise

The finance area of a business controls all monetary aspects of its operation. In particular, it considers how financial resources are allocated to different departments and ensures there is sufficient cash within the organisation to pay all its bills. At various points in the year, the finance area will report on the financial position and performance of the business.

The business's finance area will complete a number of numerical tasks and then analyse the financial reports that are prepared. For example, the department:

● organises and allocates financial resources – for example ensuring that sufficient money is given to the marketing department, production department, etc.

- reports on financial performance – it prepares detailed reports assessing profitability, liquidity, etc.
- monitors cash flow – as part of the analysis, the finance department prepares cash budgets or cash flow forecasts, in order to review the amount of money available to use.

## Staff

It is often said that a company's human resources – its employees or staff – are its most important asset. A business's success will depend on the quality of the staff it employs. For example, if an organisation employs highly qualified and experienced staff, it is likely that they will work faster and make fewer errors, thereby reducing waste.

Staff who have specialised skills are likely to provide excellent customer service to customers and ensure customers return to the business on a regular basis.

The human resources department is responsible for all aspects of managing the individuals who work within a business. For example, it will:

- plan how many staff the business may need in the future, often called manpower planning
- prepare all paperwork for job vacancies – job adverts, job descriptions, person specifications
- determine wages and salaries
- recruit and select employees
- provide training and development for all employees
- be responsible for employee welfare and motivation
- deal with employee complaints or grievances
- implement organisational policies, for example Health and Safety
- deal with dismissals and redundancies if required.

The human resources area within a business is responsible for the staff within the organisation. This includes:

- **Recruitment and selection of employees:** This includes advertising job vacancies, shortlisting candidates, and interviewing and selecting the most appropriate candidate for the job.
- **Training and development of employees:** All employees are entitled to training while employed. For example, new employees will receive induction training when recruited and then a range of other training to ensure they have the skills required to complete the job.
- **Performance management of employees:** Throughout the year, a business will review the performance of its employees. In some businesses, an employee's performance determines the amount of money they are paid.
- **Responsibility for Health and Safety in the workplace:** The human resources area is responsible for ensuring that all employees are

safe at work. They will ensure that, among other things, employees are trained in how to operate machinery and know what to do in the event of a fire.

● **Ensuring compliance with employment legislation:** The human resources area will review all current employment legislation. This includes such things as working time directives, which state the law regarding how long an employee can work during one day and how many breaks they need to take.

> ### Case study
>
> Lynne has secured a job as a barista (preparing and serving coffee) at a new coffee shop.
>
> Answer the following question:
>
> Discuss how each of the different functional areas of the coffee shop may affect Lynne.

### Motivation theory

The writings of industrial psychologists and sociologists shed light on the factors determining the satisfaction and motivation of employees. The three theorists studied in business are Maslow, Mayo and Herzberg.

### Maslow

Abraham Maslow (1908–70) put forward a theory that most of our actions are governed by our needs. He argues that we are motivated to satisfy a hierarchy of five sets of needs, shown in Figure 1.4.4.

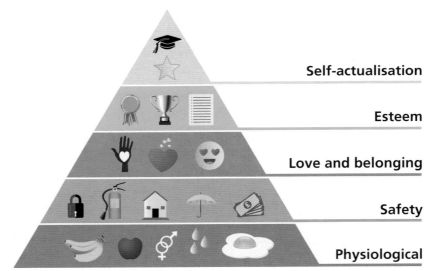

**Figure 1.4.4** Maslow's hierarchy of needs

Maslow's hierarchy of human needs spans lower-order physical needs, through social needs, towards higher-order psychological needs. Maslow believed that each need has to be fulfilled totally before the next becomes important. By the time all needs have been catered for, the individual will be motivated by self-actualisation, in other words psychological growth and development. If the threat of redundancy occurs, an individual's focus will return to basic needs such as security.

Maslow's theory has great appeal for business. Managers can find out which level their employees are at and use this to decide on suitable rewards. There are problems, however, when Maslow's theory is used in practice. Some levels do not appear for certain individuals, while some rewards fit into more than one category. For example, money can be used to fulfil basic needs but is also seen as a status symbol.

### Mayo

Elton Mayo (1880–1949) had been a follower of Taylor's scientific approach to management. He was hired by firms to conduct work-study investigations with a view to increasing efficiency – he was the 1920s equivalent of a management consultant. Mayo showed that worker productivity is influenced by far more than purely scientific factors such as tools, methods and incentives.

Mayo is most famous for his Hawthorne experiments, which took place at the Western Electrical Company in Chicago. The experiment introduced changes to working conditions, including hours of work, lighting and incentive schemes. The findings showed that no matter what changes were made, productivity increased. This was even the case when conditions worsened! The results demonstrated that employees are motivated by changes to their physical environment because of the interest that is shown by management. This interest made the workers feel valued and so increased individual morale and team spirit.

Mayo did not influence managerial techniques in the 1920s, but his findings influenced management practices such as Japanese techniques, empowerment and team working in the 1980s and 1990s.

### Herzberg

In 1966, Frederick Herzberg (1923–2000) attempted to find out what motivated people at work. He questioned 200 accountants and engineers about the incidents in their jobs that gave them strong feelings of satisfaction or dissatisfaction.

Motivating factors can lead to job satisfaction, but according to Herzberg's theory workers will not be motivated by hygiene factors such as a new carpet or a pay rise. These factors keep workers in their present job, but will not motivate them to work harder. If hygiene factors are not met, however, this will lead to dissatisfaction, which could result in a fall in productivity.

## Operational issues

The operations department deals with the production processes within a business. It is responsible for overseeing, designing and controlling how production processes work. For example, in manufacturing businesses, the operations department looks after the maintenance of equipment

Activity

## Activity

In small groups, discuss which of the four functional areas is most important to a business in its first year of trading.

Consider whether your response would change if you were discussing a business that had been in operation for 25 years.

and production lines. In this way, this department transforms business inputs, such as raw materials, into outputs that can be sold.

**Figure 1.4.5** The operations department

The operations department is also responsible for ensuring both quality and stock/inventory control. This includes ensuring that there is sufficient stock/inventory available when required in the production process. The department also reviews the logistics and makes sure that all equipment/machinery is available when required.

## Activity

In small groups, think about a car manufacturer producing cars on a production line.

**Figure 1.4.6** Cars being produced on a production line

Complete a table like the one below, detailing how the car manufacturer will use the four functional areas listed.

| Functional area | Purpose | Main activities |
|---|---|---|
| Marketing | | |
| Finance | | |
| Human resources | | |
| Operations | | |

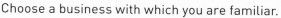

## Stretch activity

Choose a business with which you are familiar.

- Identify the key functional areas within the business.
- List the main activities completed by each functional area.

## Remember

- The human resources area within a business is responsible for the staff within the organisation.
- Maslow put forward a theory that most of our actions are governed by our needs. He argues that we are motivated to satisfy five sets of needs.
- Mayo is most famous for his Hawthorne experiments, which took place at the Western Electrical Company in Chicago. The experiments introduced changes to working conditions including hours of work, lighting and incentive schemes.
- Herzberg found that motivating factors can lead to job satisfaction, but according to his theory workers will not be motivated by hygiene factors such as a new carpet or a pay rise.
- The operations department deals with the production processes within a business.

## Test yourself

1 Write a definition of functional area.
2 Discuss the purpose of the marketing functional area.
3 Explain the role of the operations department.
4 Identify **three** key activities of the human resources department.
5 Explain the main activities of the finance department in a business.

## 4.3 Internal challenges of growth

When setting up a new business, it is vital that the owner is certain they can secure the capital (money) required to fund the organisation. This money is often used to pay for premises, equipment, machinery and advertising.

Once set up, a business will need further finance over the first few years to operate on a day-to-day basis and to grow in the future. It is very unlikely that the business will make sufficient profits to expand without additional finance. For example, an organisation may need additional machinery and extra staff in order to expand. Finance would be required to achieve this.

As the business grows and expands, there is the possibility that some customers will not pay their debts immediately, which means the business would need short-term finance to pay staff wages or to purchase additional stock to sell.

## Maintaining customer service levels

To ensure business growth, a business needs to ensure that its customer service levels are consistent and maintained. If they vary from one week to the next then it is likely that customers will take their business elsewhere, preventing business growth.

## Economies of scale

As a business grows, it benefits from a reduction in average costs of production. This reduction in costs is known as economies of scale and is what gives larger firms a competitive advantage over smaller firms.

### Internal economies of scale

Internal economies of scale include:

- **Purchasing:** As a firm increases the size of its orders for raw materials or components, the cost to purchase each individual component falls. The firm will have bulk discounts on larger orders. This reduces the average cost of production.
- **Technical:** As businesses grow, they are able to use the latest equipment and incorporate new methods of production. This again reduces average costs of output.
- **Financial:** As firms grow, they have access to a wider range of capital, which reduces the cost of borrowing for investment. Also, as assets grow, businesses are able to offer more security for borrowing, which reduces the risk to the lender and so reduces the cost of borrowing.
- **Managerial:** As businesses grow, they are able to employ specialist managers. These managers will know how to get the best value for each pound spent, whether it is in production, marketing or purchasing. This reduces the cost of output.
- **Advertising:** As firms grow, each pound spent on advertising has greater benefit for the firm.

### External economies of scale

The largest firms often benefit from external economies of scale. These include the setting up locally of supplier firms, often in competition with one another, reducing buying costs and allowing the use of systems such as just-in-time. Also, local colleges will set up training schemes suited to the needs of the largest employers, providing an available pool of skilled labour.

## Diseconomies of scale

When diseconomies of scale appear, the average costs of production rise with output.

Diseconomies include problems with communication. As a firm grows and levels of hierarchy increase, the efficiency and efficacy of communication can break down. This leads to increasing inefficiency and therefore increasing average costs. In larger firms it may be harder to co-ordinate, satisfy and motivate workers, meaning they do not give of their best. This again means that as the firm grows, the average output falls and average costs increase.

These diseconomies of scale are often qualitative in nature and so hard to measure financially, but they still reduce the efficiency of the business. As businesses grow in size, they can become increasingly difficult to control as, for example, the business may need to deal with issues such as traffic congestion, the breakdown of relationships with suppliers and buyers, competition for labour and increasing employment costs.

## Remember

- When setting up a new business, it is vital that the owner is certain they can secure the capital (money) required. This money is often used to pay for premises, equipment, machinery and advertising.

- As a business grows, it benefits from a reduction in average costs of production; this is known as 'economies of scale'.

- Internal economies of scale are classified as purchasing, technical, financial, managerial and advertising economies of scale.

- When diseconomies of scale appear, the average costs of production rise with output.

- Diseconomies of scale include problems with communication – as a firm grows and levels of hierarchy increase, the efficiency and effectiveness of communication can break down. This leads to increasing inefficiency and therefore increasing average costs.

## Test yourself

1 Write a definition of economies of scale.

2 Explain what is meant by external economies of scale.

3 List **and** describe **three** internal economies of scale.

4 Describe how diseconomies of scale affect organisations.

## Read about it

Barrat, C. and Whitehead, M. *Buying for Business: Insights in purchasing and supply management* (Wiley, 2004) – Provides answers to key questions about purchasing and supply management in organisations.

Emmett, S. *Supply Chain in 90 Minutes* (Management Books, 2004) – Provides a concise practical introduction to supply chain management.

Green, J. *Starting Your Own Business* (How to Books, 2005) – Provides a step-by-step guide to how an entrepreneur should set up a business.

Hughes, V. and Weller, D. *Setting up a Small Business* (Hodder & Stoughton, 2006) – Provides guidance and advice on how an entrepreneur should set up a small business.

Jones, P. *Tycoon* (Hodder & Stoughton, 2007) – Provides entrepreneurial examples and explains how business dreams can be turned into reality.

# Learning outcome 5: Understand external influences on business

## 5.1 External influences

All businesses are affected by external influences. These are issues that are outside of the business's control. The following would be classed as external influences that affect a business: Gross Domestic Product; interest rates; changes in the living wage; changes in fashions and trends; changes in the competitive environment and levels of employment; the availability of skills locally; and changes to legislation and tax rates.

### Gross Domestic Product

The Gross Domestic Product (GDP) is a measure of the market value of all of the goods and services produced during a period of time. GDP is a monetary value and is usually stated on an annual or quarterly basis for either a whole country or a specific region. The figure is used for international comparisons.

### Interest rates

An interest rate is the cost of borrowing money or the benefit that is gained from saving money.

- Low interest rates encourage customers to buy more goods as there is no benefit in them saving their money. When goods are purchased on credit at low interest rates, for example a mortgage, the repayments are lower, therefore businesses and individuals have more money to spend on other goods and services.

- High interest rates result in customers purchasing fewer goods as their repayments on loans and mortgages are higher. In addition, there is more incentive to save money in the bank as they will gain a higher return.

### Changes in the living wage

The national living wage is decided by the government and is the minimum amount of money that businesses must pay their employees (who are aged 25 and over). It is stated as an hourly rate and is deemed to be the amount of money required to live.

An increase in the living wage means that businesses need to pay higher wages. This means costs increase, which reduces profit levels.

At the same time, however, individuals will have more money to spend on goods or services as their earnings have increased. This means that sales could potentially increase for businesses.

## Changes in fashions and trends

Businesses need to adapt to changes in fashions and trends. A business must keep up to date with current wants or it will struggle to survive. One example in recent years is the increased use of technology. Technological developments are occurring all of the time. Therefore, any new product with electronic components needs to be able to deal with advances in technology.

It is important to remember that technological issues can relate either to the business or to the consumer. For example, most consumers want to purchase the latest up-to-date models; when new mobile phones or tablets are released, there is very little demand for the older models.

Businesses need to respond to customers' requirements and ensure they have designed new models, have trained staff so they are able to manufacture and sell the latest technology, and have the machinery available to manufacturer the latest models.

Businesses may also need to sell off at a much-reduced price any older stock that is out of date and so not appealing to the customers.

## Changes in the competitive environment and levels of employment

No organisation exists in isolation, therefore a business must take account of the current economic climate. Over time, the economic activity of a country varies, going up and down. It is recognised that the economy usually works in a cycle of decline (downturn or slump), growth, boom and recession. This can be represented in graphical form, as in Figure 1.5.1.

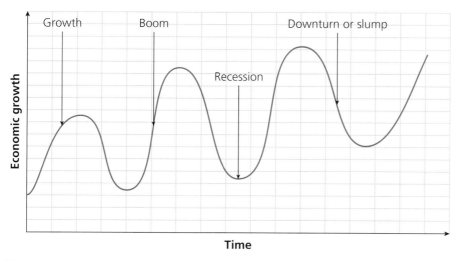

**Figure 1.5.1** The cycle of economic growth and decline

- During a decline period, businesses suffer from a decrease in sales and there is little or no demand for new products or services. A business is therefore unlikely to develop new products during this time.
- During a growth period, customers have more money to spend and are likely to want to purchase new goods or services. Businesses will therefore develop and sell new products.
- On reaching the boom period, customer spending is at its highest and businesses are likely to introduce and sell a wide range of new products.
- During a recession, customers have very little money to spend on luxury goods, so businesses need to consider developing cheaper products.

**Table 1.5.1** Levels of employment in the business cycle

| Period in the business cycle | Levels of employment |
|---|---|
| Decline | Businesses start to reduce the number of employees that they employ. As the organisation's operations are declining, so will the size of its workforce. Employees may be lost due to natural wastage, for example retirement or a new job, or there is a possibility that businesses will need to make employees redundant to save money. |
| Growth | Businesses start to recruit new employees as the organisation is growing. This means that as the business grows, so will its workforce. |
| Boom | Businesses' workforces are at their largest. During this period the organisation makes the most sales and therefore a large number of employees will be required. |
| Recession | Businesses have reduced their workforces to a minimum. There will be few people recruited. |

## Availability of skills locally

A business is dependent on the skills that are available in the local area. Organisations based in remote areas often struggle to employ high quality staff and so employees may need to be brought in from further afield. This can incur extra costs.

If specialist staff are required, for example technology experts, there is a strong possibility that employees with these skills may not be available locally. Businesses will need experts who are able to advise and implement appropriate policies to deal with these issues.

# Changes to legislation and tax rates

When developing any product, a business must comply with all current legislation. For example, products must comply with up-to-date safety standards. Laws are usually imposed by the government or national courts. Businesses are affected by employment law, consumer protection and competition law. They are also affected by copyright and patent law and taxation.

Any new legislation or change to current legislation needs to be considered by all businesses. In many cases, there may be costs involved in making necessary changes.

## Employment law

Employment law aims to protect the rights and health and safety of employees. Examples of these laws include:

- **Health and Safety at Work Act 1974:** Businesses need to ensure that their employees' health is not affected by the work they complete.
- **Race Relations Act 1976:** It is illegal for a business to discriminate against anyone on the basis of race, ethnic group or skin colour.
- **Sex Discrimination Act 1975:** Businesses cannot discriminate against the sex of individuals in their recruitment processes, training or employment.

## Consumer protection

Consumer protection ensures businesses act fairly towards their consumers. Examples of consumer protection legislation include:

- **Sale and Supply of Goods Act 1994:** This states that goods sold must be of a satisfactory quality.
- **Consumer Credit Act 1974:** This provides the consumer with protection when borrowing money or buying goods on credit.
- **Trade Descriptions Act 1968:** This ensures goods perform in the way advertised by the business.

## Competition law

Competition law exists to ensure there is fair competition within a particular industry. Governments believe that greater competition within industries will provide lower prices, better quality goods and services, and a wider range of products and services available to the customer.

## Copyright and patent law

Businesses also need to ensure that they comply with copyright and patent law. A **patent** or a **copyright** provides legal ownership of original pieces of work. When developing new products, a business could apply for a patent or copyright to ensure that its idea is not copied. The business must also ensure that it does not reproduce or copy ideas belonging to someone else.

**Key word**

**Patent or copyright:** Provides legal ownership of original pieces of work.

**Taxation**

Businesses tend to need to consider three main types of taxation:

- VAT (Value Added Tax)
- income tax
- corporation tax.

When there are changes in the taxation rates, businesses need to ensure they apply the correct rates. For example, a change in the VAT rate would mean that the selling price of goods and services either increases or decreases according to the change in the rate.

Changes in income tax affect the wages and salaries that are paid to employees. In simple terms, an increase in income tax means that employees receive less money and more money is paid to the government via HMRC.

Corporation tax is paid on company profits. If there is an increase in corporation tax rates, then more tax is paid to the government and there is less money to share out and pay to shareholders in the form of dividends.

**Activity**

Choose a business with which you are familiar.

How has your chosen organisation changed over the last few years to adapt to changes in the economic environment?

## 5.2 External challenges of growth

Whenever a business grows, there are a vast number of challenges. For example, the business will require additional resources, such as new buildings, machinery and staff. All of these cost large amounts of money and require maintenance throughout their lifetime with the business.

Businesses need to be sensitive to local cultures and legislation. For example, there can be planning restrictions on building on greenfield sites and suggestions to do so can cause massive resentment in the local area. Any increase in size may cause increased traffic, pollution, etc.

## Remember

- The gross domestic product (GDP) is a measure of the market value of all the goods and services produced during a period of time. GDP is a monetary value and is usually stated on an annual or quarterly basis for either a whole country or a specific region. The figure is used for international comparisons.

- An interest rate is the cost of borrowing money, or the benefit that is gained from saving money.

- Businesses need to adapt to changes in fashions and trends. If they do not keep up to date with current wants, they will struggle to survive.

- Over time, economic activity in a country varies, going up and down. It is recognised that economies usually work in a cycle of recession, growth, boom and decline.

- Employment law aims to protect the rights and health and safety of employees.

- Competition law exists to ensure there is fair competition within a particular industry. Governments believe that greater competition within industries will provide lower prices, better quality goods and services, and a wider range of products and services.

- Consumer protection ensures organisations act fairly towards their consumers. Examples of consumer protection legislation include the Trade Descriptions Act and the Consumer Credit Act.

## Test yourself

1 Describe how each of the stages of the business cycle (recession, growth, boom and decline) may affect the success of a new product launch.

## Read about it

Sawyer, M. *The UK Economy* (OUP, 2006) – Provides fundamental information about the UK economy.

Sloman, J. and Sutcliffe, M. *Economics for Business* (Financial Times/Prentice Hall, 2004) – Provides details on key economic topics relating to business.

Taylor, M. and Mankiw, N. *Economics* (Thomson Learning, 2006) – Provides an overview of microeconomics and macroeconomics.

**www.peterjones.com** – Provides information about Peter Jones as an entrepreneur, including short videos.

**www.bbc.co.uk/news/business** – Provides up-to-date news articles relating to business and the current economic climate.

**www.gov.uk** – Provides up-to-date information from the UK Government, including key taxation details.

**http://europa.eu** – Provides up-to-date information about the European Union.

## Assessment practice

## Section 1

1 Which **one** of the following is an internal factor for a business? [1 mark]

a Customer needs

b Increased taxation rates

c New government legislation

d Staffing costs

2 Which **one** of the following is an internal influence when developing a new product? [1 mark]

a Economic issues

b Legal issues

c Staffing issues

d Technological issues

3 Which **one** of the following forms part of the marketing mix? [1 mark]

a Cost

b Advertising

c Price

d Resources

4 Which **one** of the following is used when completing desk research? [1 mark]

a Consumer trials

b Focus groups

c Individual observations

d Newspaper articles

5 Samantha uses questionnaires to gather information for her café. What type of market research is Samantha using? [1 mark]

a Market segmentation

b Primary research

c Secondary research

d Desk research

## Answers

1 Answer: D

Additional guidance:

a Customer needs are an external factor.

b Increased taxation rates are an external factor.

c New government legislation is an external factor.

d **Correct answer:** Staffing costs are an internal factor.

2 Answer: C

Additional guidance:

a Economic issues are an external factor.

b Legal issues are an external factor.

c **Correct answer:** Staffing issues are an internal factor.

d Technological issues are an external factor.

3 Answer: C

Additional guidance:

a Cost is not part of the marketing mix. The marketing mix is represented by the 4 Ps – Price, Place, Product, Promotion.

b Advertising is not part of the marketing mix. The marketing mix is represented by the 4 Ps – Price, Place, Product, Promotion.

c **Correct answer:** Price is one of the 4 Ps – Price, Place, Product, Promotion.

d Resources are not part of the marketing mix. The marketing mix is represented by the 4 Ps – Price, Place, Product, Promotion.

4 Answer: D

Additional guidance:

a Consumer trials are used for field research.

b Focus groups are used for field research.

c Individual observations are used for field research.

d **Correct answer:** Newspaper articles are used for desk research.

5 Answer: B

Additional guidance:

a Market segmentation includes age, gender, occupation, etc.

b **Correct answer:** Questionnaires are a form of primary research.

c Secondary research involves internal data, books/newspapers/trade magazines, competitors' data, government publications and statistics, purchased research material.

d Desk research involves internal data, books/newspapers/trade magazines, competitors' data, government publications and statistics, purchased research material.

## Section 2

6 James runs a family-run butcher located in the south-west of England. There is major competition from a large new supermarket that has located on the edge of the town.

James is considering forming a partnership with his sister, Jacqueline, to try to compete with the supermarket.

  a Identify **and** explain **two** advantages of James forming a partnership with his sister. [4 marks]

### Expected answer

Advantages of forming a partnership may include:

- Easy to set up and change from a sole trader to a partnership **(1)** – there are no legal formalities involved, as there would be in the formation of a company. **(1)**
- Shared responsibility **(1)** – James and his sister will share the business responsibilities. **(1)**
- Specialisation **(1)** – James and his sister may have different specialisms, which will help the business grow. **(1)**
- Increased capital **(1)** – James and his sister can both invest in the business. **(1)**
- Holiday and sickness cover **(1)** – James and his sister can cover for each other, so the business can continue to operate. **(1)**
- Consultation **(1)** – James and his sister can discuss issues and consult with one another over business decisions. **(1)**

One mark is awarded for an identified advantage and one mark for an explanation of the advantage.

### Sample candidate answer

A partnership is easy to set up.

Jacqueline can help James with the work in the business, so he can go on holiday.

### Marks awarded and rationale

The first point is correct for 1 mark, but has not been explained for the second mark.

The second point is correct for 1 mark, and has been explained for the second mark.

3 marks out of 4 awarded.

  b Identify **three** promotional methods James could use to attract and retain his customers. [3 marks]

### Expected answer

Sales promotion techniques include:

- discounts
- competitions
- BOGOF
- point-of-sale advertising
- free gifts and profit trials.

One mark is for each method, to a maximum of three marks.

### Sample candidate answer

Offer a discount to the customer.

Provide a free gift.

Put an advert in the newspaper.

### Marks awarded and rationale

The first two points are correct, but the third point is not a sales promotion technique.

2 marks out of 3 awarded.

## Section 3

7 James is considering using either the local newspaper or a local radio station to advertise his butcher's store and to help him compete against the new supermarket.

Recommend which method you think he should use. Justify your answer. [8 marks]

### Expected answer

**Advertising in local newspaper:**

Advantages:

- Costs of advertising are low in free and local newspapers.
- Local newspaper advertising can target nearby customers, directing them to specific outlets.
- Local newspaper advertising is effective in targeting the older generation, who often read newspapers on a daily basis.

Disadvantages:

- Unless the advert is in a prime position, there may be competition for the reader's attention.
- Newspaper adverts are not targeted.
- Local newspapers are less effective for targeting the younger generation.

**Advertising on the local radio station:**

Advantages:

- Use of sounds and music can make a radio advertisement attract attention.
- Specific audiences can be targeted by choosing an appropriate station and programme on which to advertise.
- Radio advertisements can be produced very quickly.
- Radio advertisements are considerably cheaper than adverting on television.

Disadvantages:

- Radio is often used as background noise, so the advertisement may be missed or ignored.
- Prime slots in the morning or evening when people are driving to and from work are considerably more expensive than other times during the day.
- There is no way of saving the advertisement; the listener needs to take in all of the information at once.

## Candidate answer

If James advertises in his local paper, it will be low-cost. James should be able to afford this, and it will widen his target audience. This is because many people read local newspapers.

James needs to remember that not everyone in his local area reads a newspaper so not all of his target audience would see his advertisement. If James uses repeat adverts in local papers, this could be expensive and would reduce his profits.

I would advise James to advertise in the local paper as this should provide the local community with information about his store and allow him to compete effectively with the supermarket.

## Marks awarded and rationale

In this answer, the candidate talks about only one of the two methods listed in the question. This means that they can score a maximum of 6 marks out of 8.

The learner has:

- identified a benefit of James using the local paper
- made an attempt to explain how the newspaper could be used to advertise his business
- analysed the local paper as a method of advertisement.

6 marks out of 8 awarded.

# Unit 02

# Understanding resources for business and enterprise planning

## About this unit

In this unit you will learn about:
- the areas of research that businesses complete and why these are important
- how to identify and decide upon the different physical and technological resources that are required when planning for a business
- how and why businesses grow and the benefits of growth
- different elements of human resources, including the recruitment process, legal considerations and pay

- how businesses can access funding for enterprise opportunities and the suitability of these different types of opportunity
- the financial concepts that businesses use and how to calculate and interpret the different methods
- how to use and calculate various financial documents and interpret the results
- the importance and benefits of business planning and how to create a business plan.

## Learning outcomes

This unit is divided into four learning outcomes:

1 Understand research, resource planning and growth for business and enterprise.
2 Understand human resource requirements for a business start-up.
3 Understand sources of enterprise funding and business finance.
4 Understand business and enterprise planning.

## How will I be assessed?

This unit is assessed by a synoptic project from the examination board NCFE.

Through the project you will demonstrate the knowledge, understanding, skills and techniques that you have developed while completing Unit 02. The synoptic project will be set in a business situation and you will have a variety of different tasks to complete, based on the given scenario. You will complete the project in your lessons. You may be asked to plan your work in the form of a 'learner log', which will help you plan the tasks that need completing. The project is worth 60% of your final qualification and you will be given up to 21 hours to complete the work, so it is important that all aspects of the project are completed to the best of your ability. Remember that this is a formal piece of assessment so must be completed individually.

# Learning outcome 1: Understand research, resource planning and growth for business and enterprise

## 1.1 Business research

### 1.1.1 Areas of research

Many businesses are formed every year, but not all of them succeed. According to research on chain shops by the Local Data Company (LDC) for PricewaterhouseCoopers, on average 11 stores opened each day in 2017, while 16 stores closed. (This research did not include independent shops.) Do these numbers surprise you?

It is important for businesses to **research** the market that they are entering. This is to ensure they are offering something different from other businesses, so that customers will purchase the goods/services from them rather than from their competitors. Having such market research knowledge and understanding can help a business venture succeed. Several areas should be researched, including the customer base, competitor analysis, current and potential demand, and legal requirements.

### Customer base

The **customer base** is the main customers who access the products and services that a business sells. For example, the customer base who purchase holidays to ski resorts will be people who either are interested in active holidays or who like skiing. This holiday would not generally appeal to people who want to go to a hot country and relax.

In order to identify its customer base, a new business needs to undertake some research. Discovering its customer base is crucial to the success of a business – if it does not understand what its customers want from its products or services then it may produce something that is not wanted, which could result in the business failing.

> **Key words**
>
> **Research**: A method of finding out information on an aspect of business.
> **Customer base**: The main customers who access a business's products and services.

## Activity

Look at the following businesses and identify the customer base of each and the reasons why.

| Product | Customer base | Reasons |
|---|---|---|
| | | |
| | | |
| | | |

Compare your answers with those of a partner. As a pair, discuss why you think these products would appeal to the particular customers you have identified.

## Competitor analysis

Competitor **analysis** is an important aspect of business research, as it enables a business to identify other organisations that may be producing or selling similar products or services. This research identifies a business's main **competitors**, which once identified can be investigated further. The only way to ensure customers purchase products or services from the business rather than from its competitors is to identify and have information about these competitors, so that customers can be persuaded to purchase what the business is offering.

An easy way for a business to compare its product/service with those of a similar organisation is to make a competition chart. Look at the example in Table 2.1.1, for a business that is going to produce a new healthy snack bar in this very competitive sector.

### Key words

**Analysis**: Studying the results of an investigation to help come to a business decision.

**Competitors**: Businesses that produce or sell similar products.

**Table 2.1.1** Competition chart for a business that is going to produce a new healthy snack bar

| Product | Age of customers | Intended consumer: men/women/children | Price | Where purchased |
|---|---|---|---|---|
| **Humzinger** | 2–6 years | Children | £1.50 for five | Supermarkets |
| **Special K Red Berries bar** | Adults 18+ | Women | £1.99 for five | Supermarkets |
| **Nature Valley Canadian Maple Syrup bar** | Adults 18+ | Men/women | £1.50 for five | Supermarkets |
| **Cadbury Brunch Bar** | 10 years+ | Men/women/children | £1.99 for six | Supermarkets |

Looking at the chart, you can see that the products are sold in boxes of five or six bars, with all being available in supermarkets where there are several competing products on the shelves. This research may make a business consider whether or not it wants to enter into this market. These findings are an example of how competitor analysis is completed and how it is an important aspect of business research.

**Figure 2.1.1** Supermarkets sell competing products

## Activity

You are going to produce a new yogurt aimed at children. It will need to appeal to both children and parents (as they will be purchasing the product). These days, we are more conscious of the contents of processed food and the sugar content of products aimed at children, so your product will need to consider these factors.

Complete a competitor chart investigating potential competitors based on the above scenario and identify the features of the different products. Copy and complete the table below.

| Product | Age of customers | Price | Where purchased | Product features |
|---|---|---|---|---|
| | | | | |
| | | | | |
| | | | | |
| | | | | |

## Current and potential demand

Earlier in this chapter we identified the importance of a business discovering its main customer base (see page 82). Identifying its current customers will help a business know how many products or services to produce on a regular basis. For example, if a business knows that normally more people want to purchase its products or services in the summer months than at other times of the year, it can plan for this by ensuring it produces more in the summer months.

Depending on the type of business, current **demand** determines how often customers purchase the products/services. For example, if a business produces barbeques in the UK, demand for the product will normally be at the highest during the spring and summer months.

Potential demand is when a business tries to predict how popular its product or service will be to ensure that it can supply the demand. If a business has not completed satisfactory research, it could produce too much of the product or service, which will cost it money. If it does not sell the extra stock then this will also cost the business money, for a variety of different reasons:

- If the leftover stock is, for example, food items, these will have a best-before date and so be classed as perishable items. If the stock perishes then it cannot be sold and will have to be discarded, which will cost the business.
- Other stock items may have to be stored until they can be sold. If a business does not have any suitable storage facilities, it may need to rent some space. There are several different companies around the UK that offer this facility, but the business would have to decide how long it is prepared to rent the storage. This method is suitable only for non-perishable items.

**Figure 2.1.2** Companies may need to rent storage space

**Key word**

**Demand**: Supplying customers with the products and services that they want.

**Activity**

Research some local businesses that offer storage services. How much do they charge?

The risk is higher for new businesses, as they may not have business experience and may make mistakes that could be costly for the business. Therefore, it is important that the research is meaningful and helpful to the business, to ensure that it makes the correct business decisions relating to the products and services that it supplies.

## Activity

In pairs, investigate two services and three products. The products/services should include ones that are popular at different times during the year, one that is a rare purchase, such as an expensive one-off purchase, and ones that are purchased on a regular basis.

- Explain why you have selected these products or services.
- Describe why each is a seasonal, a one-off (or rare) or a regular purchase.
- Explain what a business has to do to ensure that it can fulfil customer demand.

Share your findings with the rest of the class.

## Legal requirements

The **legal requirements** that an organisation needs to declare depends on the type of business. For example, a restaurant legally requires a licence to trade. This means it must be registered and successfully complete various checks before it can serve food to the public.

Most businesses use computers, so it is important that the software packages used are fully licensed and have the required documentation. If a business uses unlicensed versions, it will be breaking the law and could be susceptible to cyberattacks.

**Business insurance** is when a business pays a company in case anything happens to it or to its employees or customers when completing its business activities. Failing to protect itself in this way could mean that the business fails. If a business employs any staff, either full-time workers or casual workers, it must have Employers' Liability Insurance. If an employee is injured while completing their job, this insurance will pay for the employee's care. Businesses that do not have this insurance can be fined up to £2500 per employee every day that the insurance is not in place. If a customer becomes ill as a result of a business's products or services, they can claim compensation. This is a payment for the distress caused by the business. Without insurance, the organisation may not be able to pay for this.

**Intellectual property law** is another legal requirement that a business enterprise must be aware of. This law protects the business in terms of its products, the designs it creates, its brand name or maybe an original invention.

All businesses are required by law to assess and manage the **risks** in their workplace. A risk is identified as something that may harm any

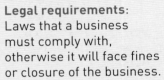

## Key words

**Legal requirements:** Laws that a business must comply with, otherwise it will face fines or closure of the business.

**Business insurance:** When a business pays a company to provide compensation in case anything happens to it or to its employees or customers when completing its business activities.

**Intellectual property law:** Protects a business's products, the designs it creates, its brand name or inventions.

**Risk:** Something that may harm any individual who has dealings with a business.

individual who has dealings with an organisation. Businesses complete an assessment of a particular situation and document this in a formal document known as a **risk assessment**.

Businesses have to prove that they have taken preventative measures to ensure that the general public, employees and any contractors do not come to harm. If you go on any trips, for instance, your school/college will have to complete a detailed risk assessment to ensure that everyone who goes on the trip is kept safe.

The Health and Safety Executive identifies that a business needs to:

- identify any hazards, e.g. steps that customers may trip on when entering the business
- decide which people might be harmed, and how
- evaluate risks and identify the precautions required
- record the findings
- review and regularly update the assessment.

**Key word**

**Risk assessment**: A formal document that businesses complete to assess the risks of a particular situation.

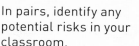

**Figure 2.1.3** A risk assessment matrix

## Remember

- Research provides a new business start-up with the required knowledge and understanding.
- Understanding whom its customers are helps a business produce products and services that will sell.
- Competition helps a business by ensuring it does not just produce the same products and services again and again, by forcing it to try and stay ahead of the competition.
- Ensuring a business can supply products and services to meet the demands of its customers is important in order to retain and gain more customers in the future.
- All businesses must fulfil legal requirements.

## Activity

In pairs, identify any potential risks in your classroom.

Describe why you think they are a risk, and what you think your school or college could do to reduce the risk.

Share your findings with the rest of the class.

## Test yourself

1 How can research help a new business enterprise?
2 Identify the customer base for a new nursery shop that hopes to open in your area.
3 Think about your local high street. Identify **three** different shops and the types of products they sell. Explain how they compete with each other.
4 Bonfire night is a popular celebration in Britain. Shops stock fireworks and sparklers for customers to purchase. How do you think a shop like Tesco ensures that it can meet the demand for the products? If it has any products left after the celebrations have finished, what do you think it does with these?
5 Why is it important that legal requirements are fulfilled by a new business enterprise?

## 1.2 Resource planning

Resource planning allows a business to identify the resources it will need to successfully start operating. Resources can take many forms, and include the physical resources and technological resources needed to supply products or services to customers.

### 1.2.1 Physical resources

### Premises

A business's **premises** can take many different forms. Businesses can be run from a room in a house, a garage, an office in a business park, up to whole buildings such as factories or office blocks. When businesses first start, they often do not have the finance to purchase large buildings, so the premises might initially be quite small and increase in size as the business becomes more successful. Having the right premises is important so that the products or service can be produced for customers. Happy customers who purchase the goods ensure that the business can continue and develop.

### Equipment

A business may need specific **equipment** to produce its products, such as machinery or specialist computers. The business may not have the finance to purchase this equipment, so it may need to hire or rent it from another business. For example, if Business A requires a photocopier, it may hire one from Business B for 12 months. Business B would supply and maintain it for Business A, meaning if anything went wrong with the photocopier Business B would send an engineer to fix it.

### Raw materials

**Raw materials** are natural resources that are used to make something new. Examples of raw materials are oil, wood, wheat and fish. Raw materials can be turned into different products and sold to customers. For example, think about milk – the business activities involved in producing the milk involve:

**Figure 2.1.4** Several activities are required to produce a pint of milk

- Farming: The farmer has to raise and maintain the cows, as well as milk the cows.
- The milk collection company: Each day the milk is collected from the farmer.
- Processing: The milk is processed and bottled.
- Distribution: The milk is distributed to shops or milk distribution companies.
- Retail: Shops or milk delivery companies sell the milk to customers.

### Transport

It is important that a business can supply its products to its customers. If a business supplies shops, large deliveries may have to be made using suitable **transport**. If its products are clothes then a lorry would be suitable, but if it is cheese being supplied then a refrigerated lorry would be needed. If the company delivers to individual customers who order online, a suitable mode of transport will be required for this. A business may decide to use the services of a specific delivery company, such as Hermes, that employs courier drivers. A business such as Amazon is very reliant on delivery drivers to fulfil its customers' orders. Deliveroo is a delivery company that delivers food from a wide variety of different restaurants and fast food outlets to customers who order online.

Customers want to receive the products that they have purchased as quickly as possible, which impacts on the delivery method used. We are now used to getting deliveries to our houses from early in the morning to late in the evening, seven days a week. Companies may charge extra for weekend or late-night deliveries, but customers still want these options to be available and so businesses must offer them.

Selecting the correct form of transport is important, as businesses do not want products to get damaged in transit to the customer. Any damages will cost the business directly, impacting on overall profits.

## Fixtures and fittings

As well as equipment, a business needs particular products in its premises in order to function. Examples of **fixtures** include cupboards on the wall or fixed to the floor. **Fittings** are items that can be moved around, such as chairs, desks and cabinets. If a business rents office space, it may be advertised as 'containing fixtures and fittings', which would mean the business would not have to supply cupboards and desks itself. This may be attractive to a new business as it might not have the finance available to purchase such items.

## 1.2.2 Technological resources

Businesses use many different types of technology to produce products and services for their customers. It is important that organisations are aware of and keep up-to-date with any changes so that they can remain competitive and provide a good service to their customers.

For customers, the methods of paying for goods and services has changed significantly over the past twenty years.

## Card and NFC readers

Most businesses have access to card and **near-field communication (NFC) readers**. NFC is also known as a contactless payment. This method works by a customer placing their bank card or smartphone on a reader, which then quickly processes the payment – it usually takes no more than one or two seconds. This is a quick and simple method of payment that customers like because of its convenience. Businesses also prefer this method, as it shortens customers' queue time.

NFC processes transactions using two electronic devices that communicate and exchange the relevant data through electromagnetic

## Key words

**Transport**: The methods a business uses to move (transport) products to customers.

**Fixtures**: Items in a business that are fixed to the wall or floor so they cannot be moved.

**Fittings**: Items that can be moved around a room or business premises, such as chairs, desks, cabinets.

**NFC reader**: Near-field communication readers, also known as contactless payment, are used to take payment from customers for items they purchase.

radio fields. Two common forms of NFC payment are Apple Pay and Android Pay, which both enable customers to purchase products using their smartphone, providing they have set up payment on their device. Credit and debit cards use the same technology, so a business can have one payment system for both cards and smartphones. This payment technology can be bought or rented by businesses. For payments over a certain amount (currently £30), customers have to enter a personal identification number (PIN) in order to validate the transaction.

When purchasing goods or experiences that cost between £100 and £30,000, customers are covered by Section 75 of the Consumer Credit Act. This means that the credit card company and the seller have equal liability (responsibility) if a problem occurs with the items purchased. It is important to remember that the items or experiences must individually cost £100–£30,000, and not be several items that add up to that amount.

## Till

Tills enable businesses to record the sales that have been made and to store money from customers who pay using cash. Tills have changed significantly over the years, from simple cash registers that did not produce receipts, to ones nowadays that record all transactions, produce receipts and are computers in their own right!

 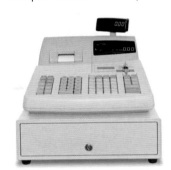 

**Figure 2.1.5** Cash registers have developed from simple older tills to modern computerised checkouts

**Figure 2.1.6** A self-checkout

Many shops have self-checkout options to pay for items. Customers scan the barcodes of the items they are purchasing and then pay for them using cash or card. Supermarkets also enable customers to scan the barcodes of items as they go around the shop and fill their trolley, and then to pay for the items at the end of the shop. Regular spot checks are made to ensure customers pay honestly for all goods.

## EPOS

**Electronic point of sale (EPOS)** includes equipment such as barcode readers, touchscreens and scanners, which record sales that are made and are a form of stock-level check. This can help businesses, because if goods are identified as running low they can order more to ensure they keep their shelves full and customers happy. Equally, if a business identifies that a product is not selling, it will know not to order any more and may introduce special offers to try to persuade customers to purchase the product.

> **Key word**
>
> **EPOS:** Electronic point of sale; used to check stock levels.

An EPOS system may also have a number of different uses within the business. If the business introduces special offers or price changes due to 'sales', the EPOS system can be set up to immediately apply these changes to the products. This system can also produce sales reports which focus on data trends related to different products, helping the business to analyse the trends based on statistics rather than predictions. Accounts reports can also be produced by the EPOS system, enabling management to have accurate data when required. EPOS systems are fast and efficient, enabling businesses to tailor the system to their requirements.

## Case study

No tills? Now that *is* smart! Sainsbury's chucks out checkouts with first shop-and-go phone scanner store.

Britain is famously a nation of queuers, but now shoppers have been given the chance to choose products, skip the line at the till and simply walk out. In a first for a UK supermarket, Sainsbury's has developed a smartphone app that allows customers to scan items from the shelves, pack them in their bag and then leave. Instead of going to the checkout, they hold up their phone to a pay point near the store exit and receive a digital receipt reading: 'You are now free to leave the store.'

After a small trial at a store in London's Euston Station, the system has been rolled out in full at a branch near Clapham North underground station in south London. Users need to download an app and link it to a Nectar loyalty card. The system uses Apple Pay to take payments. Age-restricted items such as alcohol still require clearance from a member of staff.

While the supermarket does not expect a surge in theft, and is retaining conventional tills, it will increase the number of cameras and security staff to deter shoplifters.

Source: www.dailymail.co.uk/news/article-6050757/Sainsburys-chucks-checkouts-shop-phone-scanner-store.html

Answer the following questions:

1  What do you think may be the main issues with this new system?

2  This new system will be attractive to certain customers. What types of customers will want to use this new system?

3  Who do you think would want to use the older system of queuing and paying?

## Digital manufacturing

Manufacturing has always been a vital part of business, especially planning the resources required. Businesses can now use **digital manufacturing** to apply digital technologies to the manufacturing process. This technology allows businesses to have more information at the right time. Consumer expectations and habits evolve quickly, and a digital approach allows businesses to change products faster in order to cope with the demands of their customers. A digital system means a business can easily produce a variety of designs (also known as **prototypes**) at a fraction of the cost. If a prototype is approved after testing and customer research, it can then be mass produced.

Digital manufacturing also allows products to be individualised for customers. For example, Photobox is a business that produces products using photos that customers upload to its website. Its products include mugs, photobooks, calendars, diaries, etc. Another example is a business that makes prosthetic limbs using digital manufacturing to make these specific to the individual patient. The product can be altered very quickly, reducing the time and cost for the business. 3D printing is a form of digital manufacturing that can make businesses more economical, as they can produce lower volumes and a greater range of products to increase choice for customers.

Digital manufacturing is efficient and can produce good quality products. Its more digital approach reduces the need for paperwork, which helps the business as well as the environment. The other advantages of digital manufacturing include:

- fewer errors
- quicker production rate
- reduced costs and maintenance.

The main disadvantage of digital manufacturing to a business is the initial cost of implementing such a system. This can be expensive due to the costs of the machinery required to produce the product, the training of the staff who will be responsible for the machinery and the maintenance of the new system.

## Digital communications system

We use a variety of methods to communicate with friends and family. We use our smartphones and devices to send messages and emails and 'chat' through various apps that we download. We may even message or speak through a games console. In business too, digital communications are the most common form of communication used. This is convenient as people do not need to be in the same building, city or country, which saves natural resources as flights, train or car journeys are not needed.

It is important that businesses are aware of security issues around the use of such systems. For particularly sensitive information such as customer or financial information, passwords may be put on to documents so they can only be accessed by specific people using the codes.

Systems enable communication to be electronically transferred from the sender to the receiver of the communication, and the information can be encoded digitally. For example, Tessa works in the UK and has to send a document with designs to a company in France. Years ago, these designs would have had to be sent by post, but now she can just email them to her colleague. The files are large because of the detail within the designs so she compresses the files into a zipped folder which makes them smaller in size so she can email them. Tessa then holds a videocall meeting via the internet to discuss the designs with her colleagues in France.

## IT infrastructure

Digital forms of manufacturing and communicating in business require a reliable IT system. **IT infrastructure** is the hardware, software, facilities and networks that a business uses for information to flow both within and outside of the organisation. Examples of IT infrastructure include:

- computing hardware, such as the operating systems and software used by employees, as well as the computer servers
- network equipment, such as routers for WiFi
- IT services that provide data backup, password security, etc.
- information security for the hardware and software used to protect the business, such as virus software.

The power supply to operate the systems is an important part of the infrastructure. Businesses are encouraged to use more environmentally friendly methods of power such as solar panels and solar battery systems. Many businesses invest in backup power generators to ensure that they have a constant power supply.

**Key word**

IT infrastructure: The hardware, software, facilities and networks that a business uses to enable information to flow.

### Activity

Investigate the IT infrastructure used at your school.
- What systems does it use?
- Who is responsible for maintaining the system?
- What software do you use?
- What operating system is used?
- How is data backed up?
- How is the system powered?
- What considerations are made for the environment?

Produce a report that details your findings.

**Remember**

- Resource planning allows an organisation to identify the different resources required to run its business.
- Resources can take many different forms, including physical resources and technological resources that are needed to supply products or services to customers.
- Businesses use a variety of digital methods to take payment from their customers, such as NFC readers. Digital communications systems enable communication to be transferred around the world, which helps support both the manufacturing and IT infrastructure of businesses.

**Test yourself**

1. Write a definition of raw materials.
2. Identify the raw materials required to produce fish fingers.
3. What are the main differences between an NFC reader and an EPOS system?
4. How can digital manufacturing make a business more efficient?
5. Identify the **three** different parts of an IT infrastructure used in business.

## 1.3 Business growth

Once a new business is established, it may wish to grow. Growth can be internal or external. Both are important to a business that wants to continue to succeed and develop.

### 1.3.1 Internal growth

**Internal growth** refers to how a business has grown from where it originally started to the current time, and where it strives to be in the future. This can be measured in two main areas: diversification and geographical expansion.

### Diversification

This method of growth involves expanding into new markets by developing and selling new products. A business might have a product that sells very well, and might decide to change an ingredient to make a new product. With consumer awareness now meaning businesses are focusing on the amount of sugar in products, an organisation may reduce the sugar content in its product, which could result in a brand new product being produced alongside the original product.

Fairy washing-up liquid, for example, was first sold in 1950. Under the brand Fairy, the manufacturer now also produces kitchen cleaners,

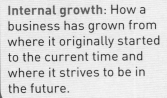

**Key word**

**Internal growth**: How a business has grown from where it originally started to the current time and where it strives to be in the future.

dishwasher and clothes-washing products. This example shows how a well-known and successful brand has diversified into new markets.

**Diversification** does not always work, however, as sometimes businesses get it wrong. In 1999, Coca-Cola launched Dasani bottled water in the USA. It was a huge success and so, in 2004, the same brand was launched in the UK. It was advertised as purified water, but its source turned out to be just tap water. The national press found out this information and the news spread quickly. Then a batch of the bottled water became contaminated and the company withdrew all 500,000 bottles that were in circulation. Within five weeks of its launch, that was the end of Dasani. Coca-Cola really did get that wrong!

## Geographical expansion

When a business first starts, it could be run from a small office in a shared building or even a garden shed. If the business is successful, however, such a location may become too small and additional space may be required in another location. A business may need to find premises to stock its products. It may then continue to expand and open more outlets around the UK and maybe eventually internationally. This is known as **geographical expansion**.

For example, a form of geographical expansion would be if a café opened on a local high street. After a year it had become so successful that it opened another branch in a different area of the town, and six months later expanded its business into the next town.

**Figure 2.1.7** Opening a new branch of a café is a form of geographical expansion

## Horizontal integration

Some businesses might want to combine with an established or similar organisation operating in the same area of an industry. This is known as **horizontal integration** and is another form of internal growth. This form of growth can be attractive because it can reduce competition in a market. There may be other reasons for horizontal integration, for example a known brand may combine with an unknown brand operating in an area the known brand is looking to diversify into.

**Key words**

**Diversification**: A method that businesses use to break into new markets by developing and selling new products.

**Geographical expansion**: When a business increases in size and requires additional premises.

**Horizontal integration**: When a business combines with an established or similar organisation operating in the same area of industry.

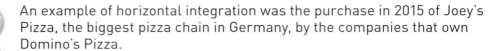

An example of horizontal integration was the purchase in 2015 of Joey's Pizza, the biggest pizza chain in Germany, by the companies that own Domino's Pizza.

## Vertical integration

**Vertical integration** is when a business that operates in one part of an industry acquires another organisation in the same industry but that operates at a different level within the supply chain. A supply chain is all the businesses involved in the different stages of producing a product. For example, the suppliers of the raw materials used to make a product, the distributors that deliver them and the shops in which they are sold are all parts of the supply chain. An example of vertical integration could be a food manufacturer and a supermarket chain combining.

Netflix is a movie and television streaming distributor service. Its customers can access a wide variety of movies and programmes using their devices. Netflix also now produces its own programmes, which is an example of vertical integration.

## 1.3.2 External growth

**External growth** is when a business grows by buying or taking over other organisations, enabling the business to expand its operations. External growth can increase a business's sales and subsequent profit, which will mean it is more dominant in the markets that it operates in.

## Mergers

**Mergers** are a form of external growth where two businesses voluntarily decide to become one organisation. This may mean that the new, merged business becomes stronger as it combines what the two businesses own, the expertise of both companies' staff, and the opportunities of new products and services. This is not guaranteed, though. Job losses could occur because staff in the both companies hold the same job; disagreements may occur due to the different ways in which the companies were run; share prices could reduce because investors may worry about the merger and want to pull out of the business, etc.

An example of a really successful merger is Disney and Pixar. They merged in 2006 and since then have produced many successful children's films. Both were successful on their own but the merger meant that they could combine the expertise of their employees to dominate a very competitive market.

**Figure 2.1.8** *Cars 3* is a successful Disney Pixar film

## Takeovers

**Takeovers** are when a business acquires control of another business. More takeovers seem to have been reported recently, because some companies have become vulnerable due to changes in the way consumers shop. As more and more consumers choose to shop online, high street shops have been seeing their sales and profits falling.

This impacts on these businesses. Some companies just do not seem as relevant and their products/services do not appeal to customers. Businesses that are relevant and able to compete against the internet markets can potentially acquire control of such struggling organisations. This can enable the successful business to grow and develop into new markets. This could increase its market share and also gain the organisation different brands to market to consumers. It will cost the business, however, as some employees might disagree with the takeover and leave. Alternatively, employees could see it as an opportunity for them personally as well as for the business.

Examples of takeovers include:

- Poundland was involved in the takeover of 99p Stores, which was making a loss. Poundland paid £55 million to take over the business in 2015.
- The Co-op bought Nisa Local for £143 million in 2017.
- Hilco, an Australian company, bought Homebase for £1 in May 2018.

## Joint ventures

**Joint ventures** are when two businesses join together for the purpose of completing a project. The businesses remain independent of each other. The project could be a long-term or short-time project. For example, a company might want to complete some research with a similar company, which then can share the findings and use them to benefit its own business. Companies might want to do this to save money, as completing something jointly means the costs are shared. Google and NASA formed a joint venture when they created Google Earth in the mid-2000s. This is still a popular resource that is used by millions of people each year.

**Key word**

**Joint venture:** When two businesses join together for the purpose of completing a long- or short-term project.

**Activity**

Individually research a business that has recently been part of a merger, a joint venture or a takeover. Explain why you think that this example of external growth occurred.

**Case study**

Read the following description of Whitbread plc, taken from the company's website:

Whitbread plc is the UK's largest operator of hotels, restaurants and coffee shops, with some of the UK's most successful hospitality brands. Our brand strength and sharp focus on markets where there is great opportunity for structural growth provide sustainable development potential for our business.

Premier Inn is the UK's leading hotel business and is owned by Whitbread, with over 785 hotels and more than 72,000 rooms across the UK. Our unique joint-site model means that more than half of our hotels are located alongside our own restaurant brands.

We also have hotels in the Middle East and Germany, with more hotels in the pipeline.

Costa is the UK's favourite coffee shop, with over 2400 coffee shops in the UK, over 1400 stores in 31 international markets and over 8000 Costa Express self-serve units. We have a multichannel strategy, with equity stores, franchise stores and stores operated by joint ventures, as well as a wholesale operation.

Source: www.whitbread.co.uk/about-us/at-a-glance

Answer the following questions:

1. Research Whitbread and identify when it has merged, taken over or been part of a joint venture with other organisations.
2. Produce an article explaining and describing what you have discovered.

## Remember

- Internal growth normally involves a business increasing in some form, for example expanding its product range.
- External growth involves increasing a business operation in size by merging with, taking over or becoming involved in a joint venture with another company.
- Merging two businesses means that the new organisation often becomes stronger in the competitive market, gaining more market share.
- Takeovers are not always welcomed by the businesses involved. Sometimes they can mean job losses for some employees.

## Test yourself

1. Write a definition of diversification.
2. Why might a business decide to expand geographically?
3. What are the main differences between horizontal and vertical integration?
4. Why might a business decide to form a joint venture with another organisation?
5. Takeovers have recently become quite common in the business world. Why is this?

## Read about it

www.tutor2u.net/business/reference/the-role-of-competitor-analysis – Notes on the role of competitor analysis.

www.bbc.com/bitesize/guides/zkr4wmn/revision/1 – Explanation of why businesses might want to grow.

www.investopedia.com/ask/answers/05/mergervstakeover.asp – Explanation of the differences between mergers and takeovers.

# Learning outcome 2: Understand human resource requirements for a business start-up

## 2.1 Human resources

It is important for companies to employ the right staff. Hiring a range of staff to complete the different roles within a business is one of the functions of the human resources department.

### 2.1.1 Methods of recruitment

When a new job role is identified, it is important that the person who is recruited has the right skills, experience and qualifications for the job. A business may decide to advertise a job role within the company (internal recruitment) or it may seek to find someone from outside the organisation (external recruitment). It could use a combination of the two to get a wider range of applicants.

### Internal recruitment

**Internal recruitment** is when a business seeks to recruit someone who already works at the company. A business may do this because there is someone within the organisation who it wants to promote. Internal recruitment means that the successful applicant will already know how the business operates and will understand the systems used. This means they can settle into the role quicker than someone who would need to learn new systems and ways of working. In this way, internal recruitment saves the business time and money. An internal candidate may not know the specific job role and will still need training, but they will already know more about aspects of the business than someone who is new to the organisation. Recruiting internally shows other employees that progression within the business is possible, which can help to motivate people. Internal recruitment is also much cheaper than other methods.

Sometimes employees want to experience working in a variety of functional areas. Transferring jobs enables this to happen, as an employee can be transferred from one function to another to develop their skills and experience. An employee's position within the business might not change when they are transferred so they may have the same level of responsibility and salary, but they will have an opportunity to find out which function they prefer working in and best suits their knowledge and skills.

The business has to decide what form of advertising to use to publicise internal roles. There are several different options:

**Key word**

**Internal recruitment:** When an existing employee gains a new role within the same business – often a promotion.

## Activity

Ruth works for a local charity and needs to recruit a manager for a new shop that will be opening soon. The charity currently has two other shops in the city. The charity cannot afford to advertise externally and would rather recruit someone who already works for the charity for the role.

Advise Ruth which method or methods of advertising this new job role would be suitable for the charity. Explain your reasons.

- **Notice board:** Job adverts might be placed on a notice board in an area where employees will see it, for example a kitchen or staff room. Employees can then easily see the advert, read about the job role and decide if they would like further information or want to apply.

- **Newsletter:** Some businesses produce a weekly, fortnightly or monthly newsletter. This informs employees about information relating to the business and is a way of ensuring all employees receive important information about the business. This newsletter could include a section where job adverts are placed.

- **Intranet/website:** An intranet is an internal website that can only be accessed by employees of the company. It can often only be accessed when you are on the premises of the business. Businesses use this system to hold information and documents needed to run the company. An intranet may also have a section where employees can view internal job adverts. As it is an internal system, any vacancies that are advertised on a company's intranet can only be viewed and applied for by people who have access to the intranet. Details about new jobs may also be posted on the company's website, which will often have a section on recruitment with information on working for the company and details of any current job vacancies. Job adverts posted on a website will be seen by people inside a business as well as outside meaning applicants could come from inside the business, too.

## External recruitment

Sometimes a business cannot recruit the right employee internally so it has to go outside of the organisation and seek an external person who has the skills, knowledge and experience for the job role. This means the business will not know the applicants' work, but will make a decision from the information that candidates provide when they apply for the job role. Bringing an external person into a job role could mean that they have fresh ideas and be really motivated to complete the job well. **External recruitment** can give a business a wider selection of people to choose from. There are several different methods a business can use to find the correct person for the job:

**Figure 2.2.1** External recruitment

## Key word

**External recruitment:** When a business recruits and employs a new person to the business who has the skills, knowledge and experience required for the job role.

- **Headhunting:** In certain areas of work, there are a number of people who have specialised skills who are known to each other. If an organisation needs to recruit a new employee, it might approach someone directly and inform them about a particular role and try to persuade them to apply. This is known as headhunting as the person is often known to the organisation through their work, and may possibly work for a direct competitor of the business.

- **Newspapers:** There are many different types of daily and weekly newspapers. Some are national newspapers that are published all over the UK, such as *The Times* and the *Guardian*, which contain national news. Other newspapers are local newspapers, which means they are produced in a local area and contain news relevant to that area. There are also specialist newspapers such as the *Financial Times* or the *Times Educational Supplement* that specialise in finance and education respectively. These are aimed at people who have an interest in the subject or work in the sector. These different newspapers each have a job section where businesses can advertise. Sometimes the jobs are classified in different areas such as education (teacher roles), medical (health care jobs such as nurses, doctors, dentists), retail (shop roles), etc. Readers can then view the advertisements and contact a company to find out more information about its advertised job role.

- **Trade journals:** Journals are often produced for specific sectors in business, such as hospitality and medicine. Trade journals contain articles and news related specifically to the sector. These articles will often feature specialists in the area of business, which will interest the intended readers but will not mean much to anyone who does not work in that sector. These trade journals will often advertise job roles specific to the field of work, knowing that the readers will have an interest. The job roles could be around the world, and depending on the trade could be very specialised.

- **Careers fairs:** In particular sectors of business, an event may be held where many similar organisations meet to advertise their job roles and give careers advice, in order to attract external applications. Businesses that attend will be given an area to advertise the company, which will often include displays about the business, employees who will speak to people attending the event, and tables with documents containing information about the business and the different job roles available. The organisers of the event may arrange guest speakers or celebrities to inspire the attendees. People may attend the event from all over the country or abroad if they are keen to work in the sector.

- **Shop windows:** Some businesses advertise job opportunities in the window of a local shop that is clearly visible to people passing by. This method has been used for decades and used to be a popular method of advertising new job roles. These days it is less popular but it can be effective, especially if the job is a local part-time role.

- **Recruitment agencies:** An organisation may choose to use a business, called a recruitment agency, that specialises in recruiting all sorts of people. The recruitment agency will have the details of many people who want to work in specific job roles and sectors of business. When a suitable role becomes available, the agency will contact potential candidates directly and forward their details on to the business that is recruiting. The agency provides a service for both parties – the business and the individual. The recruitment agency makes the money for the service it is providing through an introduction fee, paid by the company that is recruiting. This recruitment method might allow a business to quickly employ new staff.

- **Online:** Many jobs are now advertised on the internet. These advertisements can be accessed by anyone, wherever they are based. You can type into a search engine the job role that you are interested in, wherever in the world, and options will often appear. People can then find out more information directly. Some of the results will appear through a recruitment agency and others direct from organisations' own websites, which then can be looked at further. It is important for the person searching for a particular job role that they are aware of where it is based, as sometimes places have the same name but are not in the area you intended. For example, there is a place called Bristol in the UK, and also in the USA, Canada, Jamaica, Peru, Barbados and Costa Rica!

## Activity

Johnny runs a small TV production company that specialises in producing documentaries about natural history. He has to have a specialised team of film producers because of the locations they film in, as well as the time they spend abroad. He needs an additional producer and wants to recruit a new member to the team in the next two months.

Advise Johnny on the different options that he could use to find the right employee to join the company.

## 2.1.2 Stages of recruitment

Having the right employees working for a business is crucial for its continued success, so it is really important to employ people who have the required skills and knowledge for the different job roles. Businesses need to attract the best people to apply for the job roles and then, after interviewing, to offer the job to the successful person. There are eight **stages of recruitment** that a business will follow. These stages can take time, but the right person must be found.

1   **Identify that a new person is needed:** An organisation may have a vacancy because an employee has left the company, gained a promotion, retired or been dismissed, or a new job role may have been created because the business has expanded. For example, a new Business teacher may be needed at your school because more students are selecting the NCFE Technical Award Business and Enterprise because of its popularity.

2   **Develop a person specification:** A person specification is a document that identifies the skills, experience, qualifications and attributes the future employee will need in order to do the job successfully. These qualities are then split into two categories: *essential*, which means that the person must have these skills, experiences, etc., and *desirable*, meaning that it would be useful if they have these qualities. A person specification is made available to people applying for the job role (known as applicants) so that they

## Key word

**Stages of recruitment:** The different processes that a business goes through to ensure it employs the right person for an advertised job role.

are aware of the qualities required so they can determine if they think they are suitable for the role.

3  **Develop a job description:** This document states the title of the job and describes the tasks that form the job role and the responsibilities of the employee, for example how many other employees they would be responsible for, as well as whom the successful applicant will be managed by (known as their 'direct report'). The job description gives the applicant more detail regarding what the job role will require them to do.

4  **Advertise the position:** A business needs to decide if the job is going to be advertised internally or externally (see Section 2.1.1). A job advert needs to contain information regarding the job title, brief information about the job role, the location, the salary range, the closing date for applications and the email address of where to send application documents. These days it is quite rare to have to send applications by post as email is so much quicker and secure.

5  **Shortlist candidates:** People who apply for a job role will often send a completed application form or personal statement that outlines their skills, experience and attributes and why they would be suitable for the job role, along with their curriculum vitae (CV). A CV is a document that contains personal details (name, address, telephone numbers and email address) and lists the individual's qualifications and experience (past jobs), as well as providing the names of referees (see 7 below). Shortlisting candidates involves the business reviewing applications against the person specification and then deciding whom it should interview. A business will not normally be able to interview everyone who applies for a job role, especially if there are hundreds of people interested in the job!

6  **Conduct interviews and selection process:** Once the business has decided whom it would like to interview, it invites them to come in for an interview, during which it will ask them a series of questions based on their application documents (application form or personal statement and CV). The responses of the person being interviewed (the interviewee) will help the interviewers (the people asking the questions, who work for the business) decide if the interviewee could complete the job role. An interview will often be conducted by two or more people from the business, so that once the interviews have taken place, they can discuss together their opinions of who would be most suitable for the job. Second interviews may be required and the candidates may be asked to complete a variety of assessment tasks, especially for a managerial position. This will enable the business to gain further information about each candidate so that the correct decision can be made.

7  **Obtain references:** When applicants apply for a job role, they give the names and contact details of two referees. A referee is a person, often a previous employer, who will provide information (a reference) regarding the applicant's skills and knowledge. Referees may also need to provide more specific information about the individual

relating to the job role. The business will contact the referees once other stages of the recruitment process have been completed. If the references are not very complimentary about the person, a business may decide not to offer them the job role!

8 **Offer the position:** Once the interviews and the discussion between the interviewers have taken place, and references have been obtained, the successful candidate is offered the job.

Appointing the most suitable candidate for a job is really important for a business. It could be a real problem for an organisation if the wrong person is given the job, as they may not be able to complete the job role. If the person repeatedly completes tasks incorrectly and leaves the business, the recruitment process would have to start again, which takes a lot of time as well as expense.

**Activity**

Produce a poster that shows the different stages of the recruitment process, with a short explanation of each stage to show your understanding.

**Activity**

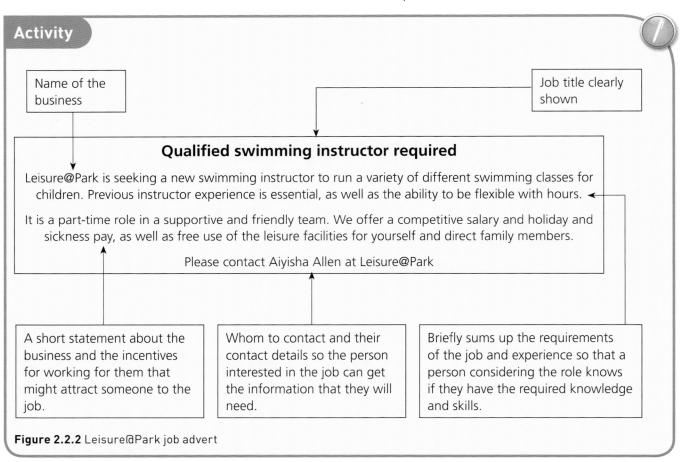

**Figure 2.2.2** Leisure@Park job advert

| Job title: | Swimming instructor |
|---|---|
| Job type: | Permanent part-time role (20 hours a week) |
| Tasks: | Preparing and teaching a variety of different weekly swimming classes for children so that they can achieve various nationally recognised swimming awards. |
| | Teach children on a one-to-one basis when required. |
| | Record attendance and achievements of each attendee and report progress to parents/carers on a termly basis using the Leisure@Park app. |
| Responsible to: | The swimming team leader. |

Gives details on whom the successful candidate will be managed by within the business.

Contains more specific information about the job role, which the applicant may want to cover in their application and might be asked about if they have an interview.

**Figure 2.2.3** Leisure@Park job description

In pairs, devise five different questions that you would ask a person attending an interview to be a swimming instructor at Leisure@Park. Why do you think these questions are suitable for the interview? Share your questions and reasons with the class.

## Activity

Produce a job advert and a job description for a sales assistant in a busy local takeaway. You can choose the type of food that the takeaway produces. Think about how you could attract a person to apply for the position.

## 2.1.3 Legal considerations
### Contracts of employment

All businesses must follow the laws relating to the recruitment of staff to ensure that it is fair for all employees. Once a person is offered a job, they will agree the working arrangements with the employer and sign a contract. A **contract of employment** is a formal document, with both the employee and the employer agreeing to the information. It contains the agreed terms and conditions of employment, including if the job is full- or part-time, the hours that will be worked, the location of the job, the pay, the holiday and sickness pay, and the holiday/bank holiday entitlement. Once the new employee and employer have signed the document, it is legally binding.

**Key word**

**Contract of employment:** A formal document with both the employee and employer agreeing to the terms and conditions.

**Figure 2.2.4** A contract of employment

Businesses use several types of contract:

- **A permanent contract** means the employee is employed by the business for an unlimited length of time. The limit will be when the employee leaves, for example because they have been promoted or got another job with a different company. Having a permanent contract offers the employee security in their job and stability for the business.

- **A temporary contract** is given to employees who are required to work for the business for a certain length of time. Temporary contracts have a start and a finish date. These contracts often are used at busy times of the year, for example in a restaurant at Christmas, when it needs extra employees. A temporary contract can often be used to fill gaps in staffing, such as when staff are on holiday or on maternity or parental leave. Temporary contracts are often for a short period of time, such as weeks.

- **A fixed-term contract** is similar to a temporary contract but it has a pre-defined start and end date. For example, a business may want to employ a person for six months as it is having a new software system installed and needs an expert to set up and maintain the system while the permanent employees are trained in its use. In this case, the business would issue a fixed-term contract to the expert. A business may also issue a fixed-term contract to cover maternity or parental leave (a temporary contract could also be used in this scenario, depending on the business).

- **Part-time employees** work only a certain number of hours per week, which will be less than a person who works for the business full-time. Part-time work is often helpful for a business, as it shows that it can be flexible, and for the employee, as it means their job can fit in with their life. For example, a person may work weekends and after 6 p.m., allowing the business to remain open during these times. This may be helpful for a supermarket that is open every day of the week.

- **Full-time employees** work a number of hours determined by the business, so it could be Monday to Friday from 9 a.m. to 5 p.m. According to the UK Government website, 'a full-time worker will usually work 35 hours or more per week'.

- **Zero-hours contracts** are becoming more common. This is when a business gives successful applicants a contract, but the hours they are required to work are not on the contract and are at the business's discretion. The hours can change each day, each week, each month, etc. No maximum or minimum hours are detailed. These contracts mean a business can offer a few days' work, for example, and the employee can either agree or disagree to the work. This gives flexibility to the employer, as it only needs to pay them when they work and does not have to provide benefits such as holiday or sick pay. If the employee constantly refuses work, however, the employer may decide that it does not want to keep offering it.

## Activity

A busy greetings-card printing business requires some new employees as it is expanding. It has realised that it needs some people all year around, as well as others at specific busy times of the year. The job roles are:

- an office manager to run the busy office
- a sales consultant responsible for gaining new customers to stock the business's greetings cards
- a Christmas card designer in the summer months to design the new cards
- a birthday card print operative to print the birthday cards
- a Christmas card print operative print the Christmas cards.

Write an email to the business manager, Brian Wilkinson, explaining the different types of contracts that would be suitable for the above jobs so that this information can be placed in the relevant recruitment documents.

**Figure 2.2.6** Job advertisement

## Activity

Office manager required
at ABC Plumbing for
maternity cover.
£25,000 pro rata with
generous holiday
allowance.
Please email
ABCPlumbing@jobs.com

**Wanted**
**Beach hut cleaners**
**in Devon during the**
**busy summer**
**months.**
**Contact David**
**on 08763 476525**
**if you are interested.**

Due to an expansion in the
business, T & J Co. require a
production assistant to work in
a busy family-run gift company.
Five days a week 9–5pm. If you
are a team player, motivated to
work hard, and want to
progress within a
successful business, email
T&JCo@recruitment.com
for more information.

**Figure 2.2.5** Three job advertisements

Look at the three job advertisements above and identify what contracts of employment would be suitable for each job, giving reasons for your answers. Your options are: permanent, temporary, fixed-term, part-time, full-time or zero-hours contracts.

## Equality in recruitment

All employees expect their employer to treat them fairly and to abide by the laws that protect both employees and employers. The Equality Act 2010 protects all persons who are in any form of employment from the following:

- **discrimination**, which is when a person is favoured over another, for example due to race, gender, disability, etc.
- victimisation, which is when a person is specifically targeted for cruel treatment by another individual or individuals
- harassment, which could include threatening, unwanted or unkind behaviour.

It is important that employers are aware that equality in recruitment also applies to disability, gender, marriage or civil partnership, pregnancy and maternity, religion or belief, race, sexual orientation, gender and age.

## Redundancies

If a job role is no longer required in a business, the person who is employed to fulfil this role may be made redundant. This can occur due to a business reorganisation, as this could mean a job that was previously completed by two people is combined into one larger job role. If this is the case, the employees affected will be offered redundancy pay. The business will offer an amount of money based on the number of years the individuals have worked for the business. The employees would agree a redundancy package with the business and then leave.

## Disciplinary action

If an employee is unable to complete the job role that they were employed to do, they could be dismissed. Examples could be because of non-attendance at work, issues with behaviour, etc. Dismissal could make it difficult for the individual to gain another job. In order for an employer to dismiss an employee, it must follow the business's disciplinary process. This will normally include these stages:

1 The manager gives the employee a verbal warning about the mistakes and this communication goes on the employee's record.
2 If a similar situation occurs again, the employee may be given a written warning.
3 A final written warning may be given by the employer before the final disciplinary process is put into place.
4 Dismissal is the final stage, where the employee is asked to leave and their contract is terminated with immediate effect.

A business must follow its disciplinary process because if it does not, the employee could take the organisation to an industrial tribunal where the case will be heard in a business court. Other professionals would then decide if the employee had been unfairly dismissed.

**Activity**

Research a case where a person has successfully won an unfair dismissal case against a previous employer. Share the facts with the rest of your class.

## 2.1.4 Staff development

It is the employer's responsibility to ensure employees keep up to date with their training, as well as giving staff the opportunity to gain further qualifications to help them complete their jobs. Staff development is good for individual employees, as it keeps them motivated and interested in their role. It is also good for the company, as these newly learnt skills and knowledge can be used within the business. In schools and colleges, teachers and lecturers go on continuing professional development (CPD) courses to learn about new qualifications or gain further understanding of the examinations and new resources to help them get the best results from their students. Learning does not stop when you leave school! There are four main forms of training and development: internal training, external training, induction and staff appraisals.

## Internal training

**Internal training** takes place at the business location, as the trainers are either within the business or come into the business. If a new piece of equipment is needed for use by a team of employees, the person responsible for the equipment has the responsibility to train team members in how to use it so they all have the same knowledge and skills. Other forms of internal training include:

- **Mentoring:** This is where a junior member of staff is paired with an experienced member of the team for an amount of time to learn new skills and knowledge. If any problems occur related to the job role, the employee can discuss these with their mentor.

- **Job rotation:** This is where an employee gains skills in different areas within the business. A company could set up a scheme where employees work in different areas for a short period of time (two or three months) to gain new knowledge and skills. This is often offered to employees who get promoted to managerial positions quite quickly, as it allows them to learn how all areas of the business operate. It could also be offered to enable an employee to determine where in a business they want to work.

- **Coaching:** This is where a specialist in a particular part of the business works with an employee for a short time, to demonstrate how to complete a specific task required by their job role, for example using some new software or making the ordering process more efficient.

## External training

**External training** is when employees go to a location outside of the workplace and receive training delivered by external trainers. This could take place at a local college or be a specialist course taught by experts from another business. An employee who has taken on responsibility for being a first aider for their business, for example, may have to go on a business first aid course so they know what to do if someone is injured at work. After the course they would go back to work and use their new knowledge and skills when required.

External training costs businesses in time and money, as employees must take time away from their job while they complete the course. The business may consider employing a temporary member of staff to cover the absent person, or may ask other employees to take on extra tasks while they are away. The employer will also have to cover the cost of the

**Key words**

**Internal training:** When employees receive training at the business location, from trainers who are either from the business or come into the business.

**External training:** When employees go to a location outside of the workplace and receive training from external trainers.

course, as it is part of the employee's development. After completing the training, the employee will be expected to use their new knowledge and skills as part of their job.

## Activity

Read the following scenarios and decide what form of training would be suitable for each individual. Justify your decisions.

- Raj has recently started at the company and is unsure how to use the spreadsheet program that the business uses. He speaks to his manager, who suggests that he needs training specifically on the software.
- David is keen to go into management, but is aware that his current qualifications and experience do not reflect his potential abilities. He speaks to his manager, who says they would support any further training.
- Patricia and her sister run a small business but want to expand to remain competitive. She needs some specific business training related to expanding a small business and wants to look at different options.

## Case study

As an employer of around 3000 people in the UK alone, Heinz has always made a significant investment in external training. Time pressures, however, mean that releasing staff to undertake courses is a constant challenge. At the same time, the company has been seeking ways to make the most of the wealth of knowledge, expertise and skills within its workforce.

Heinz introduced the concept of Learning Bitez, which consists of 1–4-hour workshops that are run internally by staff at the company. Topics range from IT skills and knowledge to can-making. They are prompted by the identification of a general need or by a department volunteering.

'The finance team discovered that the financial parts of the monthly reports often went over people's heads, so proposed a Learning Bite to explain this in more detail,' says Pat Rees, Heinz's talent manager. 'It started at our Hayes Park site, but has since spread out to other sites.'

Staff find out about the workshops available via internal communications and then book, with the approval of their line manager, through an online system. The HR department manages the booking process and deals with preparation and post-course evaluation, leaving the course leaders to focus on content.

The best measurement of short bursts of training is immediate feedback and ongoing popularity, and Rees says that both demonstrate staff enthusiasm.

'Learning Bitez have been around for a year but they have made such an impact it is as if they've always been there,' says Rees. 'There's an agility about the way the courses start and I'd like to keep this so the training is always done by someone with a passion. Internal staff know their audiences, they already know where the problems are and how they can tailor their information.'

Val Lowe is HR administrator at Heinz. 'I did the personal effectiveness Learning Bite in November. The course leader took us through the ways in which Outlook had been dominating our days and how we could organise our time better,' says Lowe.

'We looked at to-do lists and tasks, how to arrange diaries and get emails under control. I used to keep about 300 emails on my system and now I've got that down to about ten,' Lowe adds.

'I've also learned to turn off my email alert and to take a more disciplined approach by only looking at them at set times in the day. That way, I'm able to concentrate on the task I'm doing and not get distracted. I sift through and copy them into task lists.'

Source: www.hrmagazine.co.uk/article-details/learning-and-development-case-study-heinz-a-training-scheme-full-of-beans

Answer the following questions:

1 Why do you think that the Learning Bitez at Heinz have worked for:

   a the employees

   b the employer, Heinz?

   Explain your answers.

2 One of the factory sites in the UK started the concept of Learning Bitez at Heinz. Why do you think other sites might have been interested in using the same idea?

3 What are the advantages and disadvantages of completing external training?

4 How do you think that your school or college could internally train its staff?

## Induction training

When a new member of staff starts at an organisation, they are often given training to introduce them to the different aspects of the business that they will need to know. This is called induction training. A typical induction might include:

- introductions to the key members of staff that they will be working with, such as their managers, deputy managers and team
- how the business is organised, the functional areas and a history of the company
- the business policies, for example health and safety
- key expectations of employees and the employer
- a tour of the business so that they know how to get around the workplace and where key people are based
- the allocation of a mentor (if appropriate).

A business may also include specific training related to the individual's role.

The key to a successful induction is to ensure that new employees feel welcome within the organisation and have all the necessary information required for them to start completing their role as soon as they can.

## Staff appraisals

Each employee within a business will have a regular form of appraisal. An appraisal is a review of an employee's performance during a period of time, which is often each year or in some cases twice a year. Appraisals are a formal process and the outcomes are recorded. Appraisals are completed by the employee's supervisor, so if you are based within a team it could be done by your team leader. Appraisals are a positive form of development as they give an opportunity for the employee to discuss the highlights of their performance and the areas that may need improvement.

To prepare for the appraisal the employee may be asked to identify how they have achieved their targets and, if targets have not been met, the reasons for this. These can then be discussed within the appraisal process. The employee may also be asked to identify any training that they require and why. During the appraisal the employee can refer to the prepared documents and a discussion can take place regarding their targets, performance and training needs. This is then formally agreed and documents completed. These are reviewed at the next appraisal meeting.

**Figure 2.2.7** Appraisals are used to review an employee's performance

### Case study

Marco Perio owns and runs a barber's and hairdressing salon. He started his business in 2010 with his aim being to double his business. His success has meant that he is in a position to open another barber's and salon in a different area of the city. Marco has always ensured his employees are well trained and given them all opportunities to improve and develop their skills and knowledge within the business, which can then be used to train newer members of the teams. He ensures all employees know the basic skills required to work in the salon and in the barber's so that they can fill in if anyone is absent from work rather than using temporary members of staff. Marco needs more staff for the new premises. He hopes that some employees might want to apply for promotions in the business, but he recognises that new members of staff will also be required. He needs the following employees:

- a salon and barber manager
- three salon stylists
- a senior barber
- two barbers
- two hairdressing assistants to wash hair, clean up, etc.

Answer the following questions:

1  Explain to Marco the differences between internal and external recruitment methods.

2  Advise Marco what his options are for gaining the right staff to complete the different roles. What would you suggest for the different roles?

3  New staff will need to have an induction training programme. You have been given responsibility for compiling the induction day. What will the new employees need to know in order to complete their jobs? Devise the induction day, thinking about the different themes and the timings, so that they can start working at the business as soon as possible. Produce a document that clearly shows the plan for the day.

4  As the business has expanded, Marco knows that he must start to make certain processes more formal. He wants to introduce an appraisal system into the business, but he does not know what this entails. Write an email to him explaining what appraisal is and the benefits of this system to his employees.

# 2.1.5 Pay and remuneration

Employees work for a business in order to earn money that they can then use to live on. Your job role determines the amount of money that you earn. The way a business pays its staff depends on the individual business. There are different methods of pay and remuneration.

## Wages

An employee who earns a wage will often be paid on a weekly basis. The rate that is paid per hour is multiplied by the number of hours that were worked that week. All businesses have to pay the minimum wage, which was introduced by the government in April 1999. This means that no business is legally allowed to pay its employees less than the amount stated by the government. There are different minimum payment rates for apprentices and depending on the worker's age.

## Salaries

Salaries are paid monthly. The amount that someone is paid per year is displayed as an annual salary. This is divided into twelve equal payments so generally the employee is paid the same amount each month, on the same date and in the same way. If the employee takes an agreed holiday, this does not affect the amount that they are paid that month, as paid holiday is part of their contract. Knowing how much they will be paid each month can help people to budget and save.

## Piece rate

Piece rate pay is when an employee is paid for the quantity of units (products) that they complete. This method of pay means that the employee gets paid for the actual amount of work that they produce, which could encourage some employees to work quickly to get paid more – but they may not produce quality units. If the goods do not meet the required standard, this could affect the business. Think about the gift company T & J Co. (see the Activity on page 107). If these products are not good quality because they have been produced in a hurry, then customers will not be happy and not want to purchase products from the business again, which could affect its profits.

**Figure 2.2.8** There are different methods of pay and remuneration

**Activity**

Research the current minimum wage rates. There are different rates depending on age and separate rates for apprentices.

## Performance-related pay

This is when an employee is rewarded for their individual performance at work. It could be that the employee exceeded the employer's expectations and is given a monetary reward. This system of pay has to be regularly monitored by management to ensure it is fair for all the employees who are paid using this method. There is a danger that performance-related pay encourages working in a more individual way, rather than working as a team together.

## Bonuses

A bonus is an amount of money that is added to a person's normal pay as a reward for good work. A company might choose to do this at a certain time each year or if the business has done particularly well. If the business is running at a loss and cannot afford it, it would not be a good idea to give a bonus, no matter how hard the employees are working! A bonus motivates staff to keep working hard for the business and maybe remain loyal, knowing that more bonuses could be given in the future.

## Commission

In some areas of business, often in sales roles, employees are paid a basic salary and, for every sale they make, a certain percentage of the sale is also given to the employee. This encourages them to work hard, because the more sales they make, the more commission they will receive. Sometimes this form of pay encourages aggressive selling, meaning that people are put under pressure to buy something that maybe they do not actually want or need.

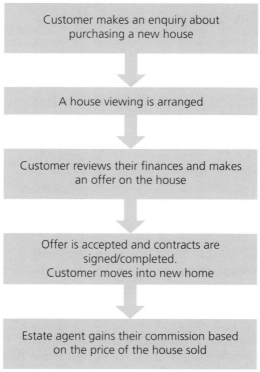

**Figure 2.2.9** An example of business commissions

## Profit sharing

Profit sharing is when all employees receive an amount of the business's profits each year, meaning that the profits are shared. The amount of profit received will be determined by the employee's job role, so a manager may receive more of the profits than a junior member of staff. If the company makes a loss, there will be no profits to share. This form of pay can therefore be an incentive and a motivator for the business.

### Activity

Looking back at the definitions of pay and remuneration above, identify which form is relevant to the following people:

1 John works in a car showroom and sells expensive cars. Each month his sales targets are reviewed and he is rewarded if he has exceeded his targets.

2 Ruby is the manufacturing manager in a large company and has to work long hours. She enjoys working for the business and has been there for five years.

3 Raj works with his family in their business. For the past few years the business has made some profits, meaning that it has expanded. As the business has continued to remain profitable, it was decided at a family meeting three years ago to change the way that the profits were used. Each family member now receives part of the profits, which they consider fairer as they all work very hard together as a team.

4 Declan delivers leaflets to 300 houses most weeks. The number of leaflets he has to deliver is different each time. For example, nearer Christmas there are more to deliver.

5 Rachel makes clocks for a local business out of recycled materials. She is paid for the number of clocks that she makes each day.

6 Eve sells office space to new businesses. When a business signs a contract, Eve receives an amount of money for her success.

7 Richard has worked for a hat-making business for one year. He was surprised when his manager told him that he would receive some extra money for his efforts. His manager was really pleased with the work that he had completed since arriving at the business and the new clients that it had gained.

### Remember

- There are two different methods of recruiting employees – internally and externally.

- It is important to recruit the right employees, as it takes both time and money for the business to complete the different stages of recruitment.

- There are normally eight stages in the recruitment process: identifying the need; developing a person specification; developing a job description; advertising the position; shortlisting candidates; the interview and selection process; obtaining references; offering the job to the successful candidate.

- The Equality Act 2010 protects all persons who are in any form of employment from discrimination, victimisation and harassment.

- Staff appraisals are a positive method of staff development.

- There are several methods of pay and remuneration, including wages, salaries, piece rates and commissions.

- Bonuses, performance-related pay and profit sharing can motivate employees to work harder for the business.

## Test yourself

1 Why may a job role arise in a business? Give **four** different reasons.

2 Complete the following sentence: The stage within the recruitment process that reduces the number of applicants to be interviewed is called _____

3 How many stages are there in a typical disciplinary process?

4 What is the difference between internal training and external training?

5 How many different forms of contract are there in business? Identify each method.

## Read about it

www.tutor2u.net/business/reference/people-management-methods-of-recruitment-gcse – Guidance on the different methods of recruitment.

www.bbc.com/bitesize/guides/zfhn34j/revision/2 – Tips on how staff are protected in the workplace, including employment rights and redundancy.

www.bbc.com/bitesize/guides/zn6hyrd/revision/1 – Tips on staff recruitment.

www.tutor2u.net/business/topics/remuneration – Links to a number of articles related to remuneration.

# Learning outcome 3: Understand sources of enterprise funding and business finance

## 3.1 Business and enterprise funding

The **funding** of any business or enterprise activity is an important aspect of business planning. As a business grows, the finances flowing in and out need to be understood and controlled, as the amounts will get larger. Large organisations have employees who work within the finance functional area who are experts in business finance, to ensure that the organisation's finances are kept in order.

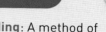

**Key word**

**Funding**: A method of gaining finance for a business.

### 3.1.1 Funding types

Companies often need to access finance to fund their business. This may be when the organisation first starts, as it may have to purchase or hire items to get up and running.

> **Activity**
>
> Jimmy is going to set up a mobile food van in his town centre. He plans to specialise in freshly made bagels, paninis, wraps and baguettes. He will also sell hot and cold drinks and freshly squeezed juices.
>
> In pairs, think about what equipment Jimmy will need in order to start his business.
>
> Share your ideas with the rest of your class.

There are many different options for business funding, providing the financial circumstances and reasons are suitable. Some may not be possible because of the situation a business is in, but other options will be available.

### Personal savings

Personal savings means that the owner uses money they have saved over the years to help fund their business. This could be a large amount or a small amount, depending on the person. This method of funding is very easy to set up because, as the owner of the money, the individual can decide how much or little is put into the business and when. The owner is in control. Using this method of funding is risky, however, because if the business fails, the money will be gone. This could put a strain on the owner and their family. It would always be advised to keep an 'emergency fund', so that there are some savings left in case of this scenario.

**Figure 2.3.1** Credit cards

## Bank loan

A **loan** is an agreed amount of money that is borrowed from a bank with an agreed payback date. The bank earns money, called **interest**, in return for lending the money to the business. The amount of interest charged to the customer is known as the **annual percentage rate (APR)**. **Interest rates** vary depending on the amount that a person borrows and the agreed time over which the loan will be repaid. The interest is paid in addition to the loan amount. A bank loan can be classed as a medium- or long-term source of finance as the payments are spread over the term of the loan. The disadvantage of having a bank loan is that the interest charged can be expensive for the business. Depending on the size of the loan, the bank may ask for some security in case the loan is not repaid. Any large assets, such as a house, are usually used for this purpose. If the loan is not repaid, the assets will be used (repossessed) against the loan.

## Credit card

Credit cards are produced by financial service businesses, such as banks. These days many large retailers offer their own credit cards to customers, such as Marks and Spencer and Sainsbury's. A credit card enables a customer to purchase items on credit. Each month, the customer is notified of the amount of credit that has been used. This amount should then be paid, otherwise interest will be added on to the amount owed each month. Sometimes companies offer an interest-free period of time where interest is not charged, but after this time interest will be incurred. A credit card is an expensive form of borrowing and should be used only as a short-term solution.

### Activity

- Research how much it would cost to borrow £5000 for two years (24 months) from three different companies. What are the differences in the interest rates they charge? How much in total will you repay over the period of the loan, including interest?
- Research the interest rates of three different credit cards. Work out how much interest you would pay if you borrowed £1000 over two years.

## Loan from family and friends

This is when a business is funded by friends and family of the owner. Like a bank loan, it is money that is borrowed for a period of time and agreed by the parties involved. It would be advised to document the amounts involved and the agreed payback dates so that this does not cause any disagreements later on. It is a risk borrowing from friends and family, as like with any loan, if the business fails the finance still needs to be repaid.

## Prince's Trust loan

The Prince's Trust was set up in 1976 by HRH the Prince of Wales to deliver and commit to 'improving the lives of disadvantaged young people in the UK' (source: www.princes-trust.org.uk/about-the-trust/history). Over the years, 825,000 young people have been helped in numerous ways by the charity, from attending training courses, completing qualifications, gaining jobs and accessing funding. The Prince's Trust supports new businesses with start-up loans of up to £5000. Like other loans, the amount is paid off monthly, with agreed interest for the duration of the loan. Look at the Prince's Trust website and see what it offers young people. You may be surprised! www.princes-trust.org.uk

### Activity

Since 1976, the Prince's Trust has helped thousands of young people set up successful businesses.

Go to www.princes-trust.org.uk/about-the-trust/history and research this important charity. Identify how it has helped young people and the impact that it has had on their lives.

Share your findings with the rest of your class.

## Grants

**Grants** are a form of funding that is supported and funded by the government. The government enables small businesses that meet specific criteria to apply for grants of between £500 and £500,000. Small businesses may be eligible for grants, whether they are new, developing or established. As well as offering access to business funding, the government also offers support to businesses in the form of knowledge and expertise.

### Key word

**Grant:** Funding provided and supported by the government to help small businesses.

## Credit agreements

When any form of credit funding is taken out by a business, an agreement of the specific details (also known as the terms and conditions) is documented, with both parties being given copies of the documents. The terms and conditions detail the amount of credit, the duration of the credit, the interest to be charged, what will happen if payments are not made, etc. It is a legally binding document.

## Business Angels

Business Angels are often individuals who have wealth and an entrepreneurial mind, who are willing to take risks in order to own a proportion of a business. They effectively invest money in a new business venture, in the hope that it will be successful. The popular BBC programme *Dragons' Den* is a good example of people investing and taking risks by backing new businesses. The Business Angel will often have expertise in business, which could be very useful to a new business. Some Business Angels want to be involved in the organisation, whereas others just want to invest. Either way, the Business Angel will own part of the business.

## Overdrafts

Overdrafts are a short-term source of finance. These are when a bank allows a business to withdraw money from its account, up to an agreed amount, even if it does not have the balance in its account. Any money withdrawn that was not in its account is then known as 'overdrawn' and the business is using their agreed overdraft. Banks often charge their customers for having an overdraft option. Banks also set a limit to the overdraft that can be used, such as £200 per customer.

For example, a business has £50 in its account and an agreed overdraft of £250. The business receives a bill for £75. It pays this bill, meaning its new balance is £25 overdrawn. The business then receives £25 into its account. Its balance is now £0 as it has paid the overdrawn amount back to the bank.

## Crowdfunding

**Crowdfunding** involves many different people giving money, often for the purpose of starting a new project. People donate small amounts of money, normally online, which can generate publicity for the new project or business as more people give money. Targets can be set and often are quickly achieved as awareness grows. There are different types of this form of funding, including:

- **Donation-based:** When you donate to a charity or a person, but you do not expect to get anything in return for your donation.
- **Investment-based:** When you invest in a business and receive something in return for your investment.
- **Loan-based:** When you loan an amount of money and the person receiving the money pays it back with interest.

Crowdfunding isn't regulated in the same way as bank loans, so there is a risk for the investors. Crowdfunding has become popular over the past five years. The tennis player Andy Murray invested in three different companies using crowdfunding, according to the *Telegraph*, saying that, 'The three businesses I've chosen are all in areas of industry I find interesting.' (Source: **www.telegraph.co.uk/finance/personalfinance/investing/12005303/First-crowdfunding-results-70-go-bust-one-makes-money.html**).

## Trade credit

Trade credit is when credit is given to a business for an agreed amount of time, such as 30, 60 or 90 days. The balance must be paid within the agreed timescale. The business (which is known as 'trade') would be offered this credit by companies that they use on a regular basis. It is a short-term funding option. Sometimes businesses receive special offers for their regular custom. An example would be a plumber who regularly buys materials from a specific supplier, which offers the plumber trade credit.

**Figure 2.3.2** Andy Murray has invested in crowdfunded businesses

## Remember

- There are different short-term and long-term funding options for businesses.
- Some financial institutions require security as part of any contract. Security is often a house.
- A business needs to carefully consider what form of financial funding will be manageable.
- Interest rates vary according to the type of funding.
- Having an emergency fund of savings is important, in case anything goes wrong with the business.

## Test yourself

1. Name **four** types of funding that a business could access and describe each one.
2. Why is it risky to fund a business using your personal savings?
3. What is the difference between an overdraft and a bank loan?
4. Write a definition of crowdfunding.
5. Complete the following sentence: HRH the Prince of Wales set up the _____ in 1976. Why did he set this up?
6. Why is a credit agreement an important document and what information should it contain?

## 3.2 Business and enterprise finance

Once a business has been able to fund its operations, it must keep records of all financial transactions, as these will need to be documented. Imagine if you sold a number of different items in a week, but did not record when they were purchased, what was specifically purchased and how much you charged the customers. How would you know? Keeping financial records is vital so that you know how much stock you had to start with, how much you have sold and the selling prices. This will help you track your sales and to work out if any profit has been made.

### 3.2.1 Financial concepts and calculations
#### Income statement

Each year a business is required to produce an **income statement**. The income statement details the revenue (the money) that comes into the business from the sales of products or services, as well as the expenses that the business has used. Expenses are the money the business spent to make the products or services, such as the materials, the heat and light used within the business, the rent, etc. The income statement shows all this information in one document and then calculates the profit or loss the business has made during the year. It enables a business to look at its

**Key word**

**Income statement:** Details the revenue (the money) that comes into a business from the sale of products or services, as well as the expenses that the business has used.

**Activity**

Write down a list of expenses that you think a small milkshake business uses. Compare your answers with the rest of your class.

performance during the year. A financial year is not the same as a calendar year – the financial year starts on 6 April and ends on 5 April each year.

An income statement is presented in a particular way. The layout is important for the business, as it must be simple and show the sales and expenses as well as two other important figures.

For example, Party Plus produces a wide variety of products for any celebration, from birthdays to Easter, Eid, Christmas, etc. Each year it produces an income statement that details the profit or loss made.

### Income statement for Party Plus

|  | £ |
|---|---|
| Sales revenue | 175,400 |
| Less costs of sales | 97,700 |
| **Gross profit** | **77,700** |
| Less expenses | 48,200 |
| **Net profit** | **29,500** |

**Figure 2.3.3** An income statement for Party Plus

This basic income statement shows that Party Plus's sales revenue was £175,400, meaning that it sold this value of goods over the year. It can only know this by keeping receipts and records of each sale. The costs of sales on the income statement is the amount that it cost the business to make all of the products it produced and sold. These costs include the materials to make the products. The costs of sales is deducted from the sales revenue, which then displays the gross profit, which for Party Plus is £77,700. Gross profit is the profit before expenses are taken off the total, and is the first **main** figure shown on the income statement.

The next part of the income statement is where the expenses are added up and then deducted from the gross profit. As Figure 2.3.3 is a basic example of an income statement, a total figure of £48,200 is shown for expenses. More detailed income statements detail what specific expenses could be, such as rent, wages/salaries, etc. (e.g. see Figure 2.3.12 on page 133).

The expenses are then deducted from the gross profit, to give the business's overall net profit figure. This is the money that the business has access to after all costs and expenses have been deducted. This shows the business how much profit it has earned during the financial year and it can then decide what to do with the profit.

## Impact of income statement on a business

Having an income statement means that a business can compare these calculations over time and analyse the changes in revenue and expenses. This allows it to alter its business methods accordingly. For Party Plus, for example, if the costs of making bunting increased, this cost may have to be passed on to customers through increased prices. This may affect sales, so Party Plus may consider changing to a cheaper form of materials to produce the bunting. This is an example of changing a business method.

Collating its sales revenue allows Party Plus to identify which products were most popular and least popular. It may decide to change the types of products it stocks or to advertise particular products more prominently to try to increase the sales.

### Activity

Braken Plants has a small market stall. It goes around various markets in Northamptonshire each weekday to sell its seasonal plants. It is preparing its income statement and needs some help working out its sales. It has kept a record of each month's sales at the different markets, which are shown in the table below:

| Month | Sales (£) |
|---|---|
| April | 1500 |
| May | 1700 |
| June | 3000 |
| July | 2000 |
| August | 2500 |
| September | 1900 |
| October | 1500 |
| November | 1400 |
| December | 1000 |
| January | 1000 |
| February | 1200 |
| March | 1400 |

- Work out the sales revenue for Braken Plants.
- The costs of sales is £200 each month. Calculate the costs of sales for the year.
- Using the sales revenue figure and costs of sales calculation, calculate the overall gross profit for Braken Plants.

## 3.2.2 Costs, liabilities and assets

We have established the importance for a business of keeping financial records, as it ensures all the costs that are made or received by the business can be tracked and then documented. There are many different costs to a business throughout its life, from the very beginning, as it grows, if it changes direction or if it decides to end. Costs may go up, go down or just change with the business.

## Start-up costs

When a business first starts, it will have start-up costs. These costs affect a new business because it has to purchase specific items before it can begin producing products or services. Think about the Activity on page 117 where you wrote a list of equipment Jimmy would need to set up a mobile food van and start trading. The purchase of these items would form part of his start-up costs.

The start-up costs for each business will be different as they depend on what the business is selling to its customers. If the new business was offering a service, such as a vet, it would need premises, office furniture, IT equipment, staff, etc. A shop would have to purchase stock, have the right fixtures and fittings to display the goods, and have premises and IT equipment. A new manufacturer would have large costs for a factory, such as machinery, equipment, tools, parts, etc. All these costs have to be covered, forming the start-up costs for the business.

## Running costs

Running costs are costs to keep the business operating or running. They are the everyday costs that have to be paid all the time, and include rent, wages and salaries, insurance, electricity and gas, telephone and broadband charges, etc. Some costs alter each month, for example in the winter the business may use more electricity and gas to heat the premises. At busy times of the year, the business may have higher wages to pay if it needs to take on more staff on a temporary basis to meet the customer orders.

## Fixed costs

Some of the running costs a business has to pay will not change; these are called fixed costs. These have to be paid every month, no matter whether the business has a good or a bad month of sales. Examples of fixed costs include:

**Figure 2.3.4** Examples of fixed costs

- rent
- loan repayments
- advertising
- insurance, e.g. of the buildings and the building contents
- salaries
- utilities, e.g. electricity, water.

A graph of fixed costs would be a straight line, as shown in Figure 2.3.5. Remember that fixed costs do not change (increase or decrease) if the output from a business changes.

## Variable costs

Variable costs change according to a business's level of output. For example, if 50 items are made and then another 20 are needed, the business will need to order in more materials to make the products. The raw materials and manpower that are used to make the extra output are examples of variable costs. Other examples of variable costs include:

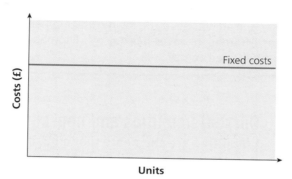

**Figure 2.3.5** Graph of fixed costs

- **Stock:** Also known as inventory, this is the goods or items that a business keeps in its shop or warehouse for sale to its customers. For example, a sandwich shop may have stock of bags of crisps and bottles of drink.
- **Components:** These are parts that make up a whole item. For example, flour would be a component in making a bread roll.
- **Packaging costs:** These are the costs of packaging the finished products. For example, the costs of putting sandwiches into boxes for sale.

In a clothes factory, if production of clothing doubles then the variable costs double; if production of clothing halves, the variable costs halve; if output is zero, then no variable costs are incurred.

$$\text{Total variable costs} = \text{variable cost per unit} \times \text{output level}$$

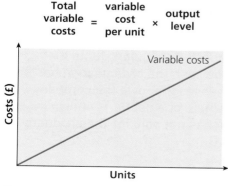

**Figure 2.3.6** Graph of variable costs

## Activity

Sarah sells ice lollies in the summer at an outdoor swimming pool. On a busy day she can sell up to 300 lollies, each for £1.50. Her total revenue on a busy day when she sells out of lollies is: 300 × £1.50. Therefore her total revenue is: £450.

Sarah has to pay £20 in rent each day that she sells her lollies at the pool. She works six days a week. The rent covers the electricity needed to keep the lollies frozen. This cost does not change, so on days when there are not that many people swimming, she makes fewer sales but still has to pay the £20 rent.

- Identify the fixed costs in the above case study.
- How much does Sarah pay each week for her fixed costs? Calculate this total.
- The swimming pool has decided to charge Sarah a weekly rent of £150 instead of a daily rate. It is also going to charge her a daily electricity charge, as there have been recent increases to this cost. This charge will be £3.00 per day. Sarah will be at the swimming pool six days a week and will have one day off. She will employ her brother, Thomas, to cover her day off. Thomas will be paid £45 for the day. How much will she now have to pay for her fixed costs?

## Key words

**Liabilities**: Debts that a business may have incurred while trading.

**Assets**: Resources that a business owns so that it can operate.

## Current liabilities and non-current (long-term) liabilities

**Liabilities** are the debts that a business may have incurred while trading. It is not unusual for businesses to have liabilities, as they cannot own everything unless they have an endless supply of money!

Some liabilities are short term, for example a builder may have 60 days to repay the credit for building materials purchased. These short-term liabilities/debts are known as current liabilities. Long-term liabilities are debts that are going to take much longer to pay, such as a bank loan or mortgage, which could take years to repay. Long-term liabilities are debts that will take more than 12 months to pay off.

## Current and non-current (fixed) assets

**Assets** are the different resources that a business owns so that it can operate. Have you ever heard the expression 'You're a real asset'? It means that you add value, just like an asset in business terms. Like liabilities, assets fall into two separate categories:

- Non-current (fixed) assets are resources that are used again and again to help the business function and survive. Examples would be machinery, vehicles and premises.
- Current assets are items that can be quickly turned into cash, if required. Examples could be the business's stock (products that are already made that can be sold), the cash the organisation has in the bank, and the individuals or businesses that owe the company money (known as its debtors). An example of a debtor is shown in Figure 2.3.7, which shows Company A has not paid for the products that it has purchased from Company B.

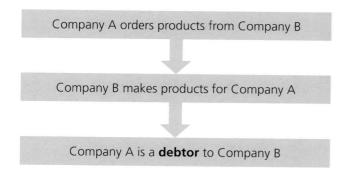

Company A orders products from Company B

Company B makes products for Company A

Company A is a **debtor** to Company B

**Figure 2.3.7** How a company can become a debtor

Answer the following questions:

1  Are running costs and start-up costs the same? Explain your answer.
2  True or false: Paying the rent for premises is an example of a variable cost.
3  An example of a start-up cost is _____
4  Stock can be quickly turned into what?
5  What is the difference between liabilities and assets?
6  What are the **two** different types of liabilities?
7  Would a two-year bank loan be a current liability or a non-current (long-term) liability?

## 3.2.3 Financial documents

We have established the importance of businesses keeping good records of all financial transactions. This enables important figures to be used to analyse the business's performance and adjustments to be made to the way that the organisation operates. For example, if sales are slow during the summer months, more advertising could take place with special introductory customer discounts given to try to generate more sales.

### Break-even chart

We saw in Unit 01 Section 1.2.1 how the break-even point is calculated. Break-even is when the costs that a business generates are the same as its sales revenue. Break-even can be written in as a formula:

**Total revenue = Total costs**

For example, a business sells its product for £4.00 per unit. The business's total costs are £20,000 (fixed costs plus total variable costs). Therefore, the business knows that it has to sell 5000 units at £4.00 per unit to break even (5000 × £4.00 = £20,000).

If the business sells 5001 units, it will make a profit; if it sells 4999 products, it will make a loss. (Remember: the business makes neither a profit nor a loss at the break-even point.)

To work out the break-even point you need to have access to the following costs:

- fixed costs
- variable costs per unit
- selling price per unit.

The formula to calculate the break-even point is:

$$\textbf{Break-even point} = \frac{\textbf{Fixed costs}}{\textbf{Selling price per unit} - \textbf{Variable cost per unit}}$$

For example, a local charity band wants to encourage people to download its latest music release. It needs to work out the break-even point so it knows when it will be making a profit, which it will then donate to its chosen charity. Its fixed costs are £600; the selling price per unit is 35p; the variable costs per unit are 20p. Using the equation above, it has worked out the following:

$$\textbf{Break-even point} = \textbf{£600 / (35p – 20p)}$$

$$= \textbf{£600 / 15p}$$

$$= \textbf{4000 downloads before it breaks even}$$

## Activity

Using the break-even point formula, complete the following table to calculate the break-even point of various stationery items.

|  | Pens | Books | Pencils | Folders | Staplers |
|---|---|---|---|---|---|
| **Fixed costs** | £45,000 | £100,000 | £20,000 | £10,000 | £50,000 |
| **Price per unit** | £2.00 | £15.00 | £1.00 | £3.00 | £4.00 |
| **Variable costs per unit** | £0.50 | £7.00 | £0.20 | £1.00 | £1.50 |
| **Break-even point** |  |  |  |  |  |

- If the fixed costs were to increase by 10% for each item, what do you think would happen to the break-even points?
- Why might the fixed costs increase for a business?

Some businesses like to present their break-even in graphical form, known as a break-even chart. A break-even chart shows the lines of fixed costs, total costs and total revenue at each point of output. The chart can plot the break-even point as this is when the total revenue and the total costs lines cross.

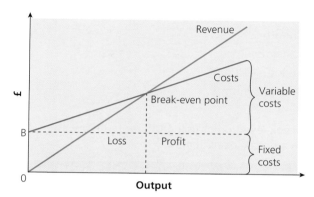

**Figure 2.3.8** A break-even chart (Source: www.tutor2u.net/business/reference/breakeven-point)

For example, Bailey Brown makes small garden tables. His fixed costs are £20,000 and variable costs are £10 per unit. The selling price for each unit is £60. His aim is to break even as quickly as possible.

The table in Figure 2.3.9 shows how Bailey can work out his break-even point.

| Number of tables sold | 100 | 200 | 300 | 400 | 500 |
|---|---|---|---|---|---|
| Fixed costs | 20 000 | 20 000 | 20 000 | 20 000 | 20 000 |
| Variable costs | 1000 | 2000 | 3000 | 4000 | 5000 |
| Total costs | 21 000 | 22 000 | 23 000 | 24 000 | 25 000 |
| Sales revenue | 6000 | 12 000 | 18 000 | 24 000 | 30 000 |
| Break-even point | | | | | |

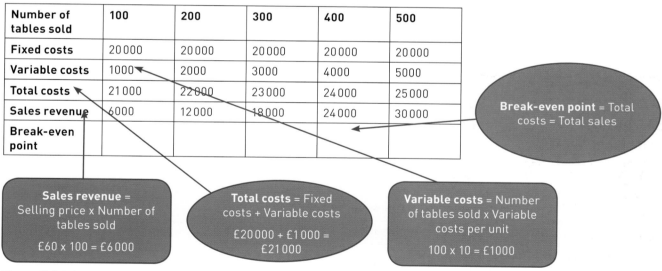

**Figure 2.3.9** Calculating Bailey's break-even point

Sales revenue =
Selling price x Number of tables sold

£60 x 100 = £6000

Total costs = Fixed costs + Variable costs

£20 000 + £1 000 = £21 000

Variable costs = Number of tables sold x Variable costs per unit

100 x 10 = £1000

Break-even point = Total costs = Total sales

## Activity

Using the figures for Bailey Brown's garden tables above, create a break-even chart that identifies the number of tables he needs to sell in order to break even.

**Case study**

A retro adventure gaming company is producing model kits of its characters for model enthusiasts to purchase and make. It wants to work out how many kits it needs to sell so that it can set its sales team realistic targets.

● Fixed costs are £800 per month.
● Variable costs are £4.00 per unit.
● Selling price of each model kit is £20.00.
● It thinks it might sell 150 kits per month.

Answer the following questions:

1 Work out the company's break-even point using the table below, then present this information in a break-even graph.

| Number of kits | 0 | 25 | 50 | 75 | 100 | 125 | 150 |
|---|---|---|---|---|---|---|---|
| Fixed costs | | | | | | | |
| Variable costs | | | | | | | |
| Total costs | | | | | | | |
| Sales revenue | | | | | | | |

Explain how you worked out the break-even point.

2 The fixed costs increase by £100 each month. What effect will this have on the break-even point?

3 What should the business do to ensure its profit margins do not decrease with the increase in fixed costs?

4 What might be the effect of the action you identified in question 3 on the business? Explain your answer.

**Key word**

**Cash flow forecast:** A prediction of what may or may not happen within a year for a business, by predicting the flow of money coming into and out of the business.

## Cash flow forecast

The flow of money coming into and out of a business can be documented in a **cash flow forecast**. This is an accounting tool used to budget and forecast what may happen with a business during a year, from January to December. Money flowing into the business is from selling products and services. Money flowing out of the business is when the business pays for items such as rent.

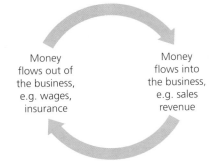

Money flows out of the business, e.g. wages, insurance

Money flows into the business, e.g. sales revenue

**Figure 2.3.10** Money flowing into and out of a business

All these separate items are recorded on a cash flow forecast, which businesses use to identify issues that may occur, hopefully before they happen, and to plan for future projects, such as expanding the business using the finance from the profits. If the business identifies issues that may occur, it can try to avoid these by planning ahead. An example could be increasing sales in busy periods to cover the times when sales are lower, or reducing the business's costs each month.

The T-shirt Company has started to compile a cash flow forecast. It is a local family-run business that would like to expand its operations in the next five years, so this document is very useful for its planning.

Opening balance is the amount of money that a business has at the start of the month

Total cash inflows is the amount of money that the business expects to receive during the month

Total cash outflows is the amount of cash that the business will pay out

| | Jan (£) | Feb (£) | Mar (£) |
|---|---|---|---|
| **Opening balance** | 10,000 | 62,800 | 134,100 |
| **Cash inflows** | | | |
| Sales revenue | 60,000 | 65,000 | 70,000 |
| Loan | 5000 | 5000 | 5000 |
| Sale of van | | 14,000 | |
| **Total cash inflows** | 65,000 | 84,000 | 75,000 |
| | | | |
| **Cash outflows** | | | |
| Materials | 3000 | 3500 | 4000 |
| Wages | 8000 | 8000 | 8000 |
| Rent | 1000 | 1000 | 1000 |
| Other expenses | 200 | 200 | 200 |
| **Total cash outflows** | 12,200 | 12,700 | 13,200 |
| | | | |
| **Inflow – Outflow** | 52,800 | 71,300 | 61,800 |
| **Closing balance** | 62,800 | 134,100 | 195,900 |

Inflow – Outflow is the difference between the money coming into and out of the business: **£65,000 – £12,200 = £52,800**

Closing balance is worked out by adding the opening balance figure to the inflow – outflow figure. The closing balance is **£10,000 + £52,800 = £62,800**. This figure then becomes the opening balance for the next month of February

**Figure 2.3.11** A cash flow forecast

## Activity

Complete the table below:

| | Explanation of term |
|---|---|
| **Cost per unit** | |
| **Profit per unit** | |
| **Total costs** | |
| **Total profit** | |

● Identify two examples of fixed costs and two examples of variable costs.
● Write a definition of break-even.
● How is break-even calculated?
● How can break-even help a business?

## Case study

Robertson's Records has been open for many years. With the recent trend of records becoming more popular, it has seen an increase in profits over the past year. It is even considering stocking record players for customers to purchase, but it needs to see if this is a viable option.

Help it compile a cash flow forecast for the first five months of the year.

| | January | February | March | April | May |
|---|---|---|---|---|---|
| **Opening balance** | 12,000 | | | | |
| | | | | | |
| **Cash inflows** | | | | | |
| **Sales revenue** | 34,000 | 36,000 | 41,000 | 20,000 | 36,000 |
| **Loan** | 1000 | 1000 | 1000 | 1000 | 1000 |
| **Total inflows** | | | | | |
| | | | | | |
| **Cash outflows** | | | | | |
| **Equipment** | 5000 | | | | |
| **Stock** | 20,000 | 24,000 | 24,000 | 28,000 | 29,000 |
| **Rent** | 2000 | | | | |
| **Salaries** | 6000 | | | | |
| **General expenses** | 1000 | 1000 | 1000 | 1000 | 1000 |
| **Total outflows** | 34,000 | | | | |
| | | | | | |
| **Total inflows – Total outflows** | | | | | |
| **Closing balance** | | | | | |

Answer the following questions:

1 Calculate the total inflows for January to May.
2 Work out the Total inflows – Total outflows.
3 Calculate the closing balance for January.
4 Add in the opening balance for February.
5 Add in a monthly rent of £2000 as well as a salaries cost of £6000 for each of the remaining months.
6 Calculate the Total inflows – Total outflows for the remaining months, as well as the closing balances and opening balances.

## Income statement (profit and loss account)

In Section 3.2.1 we looked at a basic income statement. The income statement details the revenue (the money) that comes into the business from the sales of products or services, as well as the expenses that the organisation used during the financial year. The two key figures in an income statement are the gross profit (calculated from the money coming into the business, for example from sales revenue) and the net profit (the profit once expenses have been taken off the gross profit figure). The income statement helps a business determine how it is performing, by identifying if it is making a profit or a loss. The income statement might also be called the profit and loss account.

**Gross profit** is calculated by using the sales revenue figure and subtracting from this the cost of sales.

The gross profit for Hot Drinks For You is £57,000.

**Net profit** is calculated by taking the gross profit figure and subtracting from this the total expenses figure.

The net profit for Hot Drinks For You is £34,100.

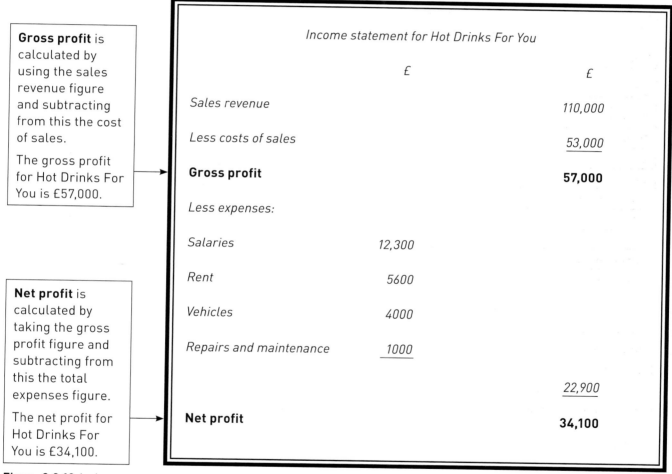

Income statement for Hot Drinks For You

| | £ | £ |
|---|---|---|
| Sales revenue | | 110,000 |
| Less costs of sales | | 53,000 |
| **Gross profit** | | **57,000** |
| Less expenses: | | |
| Salaries | 12,300 | |
| Rent | 5600 | |
| Vehicles | 4000 | |
| Repairs and maintenance | 1000 | |
| | | 22,900 |
| **Net profit** | | **34,100** |

**Figure 2.3.12** An income statement

## Activity

Financial information about a business is given below.

| | | | |
|---|---|---|---|
| Sales | £156,400 | Equipment | £150 |
| Cost of sales | £80,200 | Uniforms | £100 |
| Rent | £20,000 | General expenses | £7000 |
| Advertising | £7000 | Computers | £300 |

- Prepare an income statement for Mirsa Johns, the owner of the business.
- What is her gross profit?
- What items could be included in her general expenses?
- What is the business's net profit?

**Key word**

**Statement of financial position**: A snapshot of a company's assets and liabilities at a particular point within the financial year.

## Statement of financial position (balance sheet)

A **statement of financial position** is a useful document for a business to compile, as it gives a snapshot of the company's assets and liabilities at a particular point in the financial year. This tells the company how much it is worth. The statement of financial position might also be called the balance sheet. There are three main parts to the statement of financial position:

- Section 1 – The assets
- Section 2 – The liabilities
- Section 3 – The capital and reserves that the business may or may not have.

These documents are accessed by stakeholders in the business. People who have a vested interest in the performance of the organisation, for example shareholders, banks or employees, might also be interested to see how the business is doing. A statement of financial position should balance, as the value of a business's assets is exactly the same as its liabilities and capital added together. If it does not balance then there is a problem. See the example below for Fans Limited.

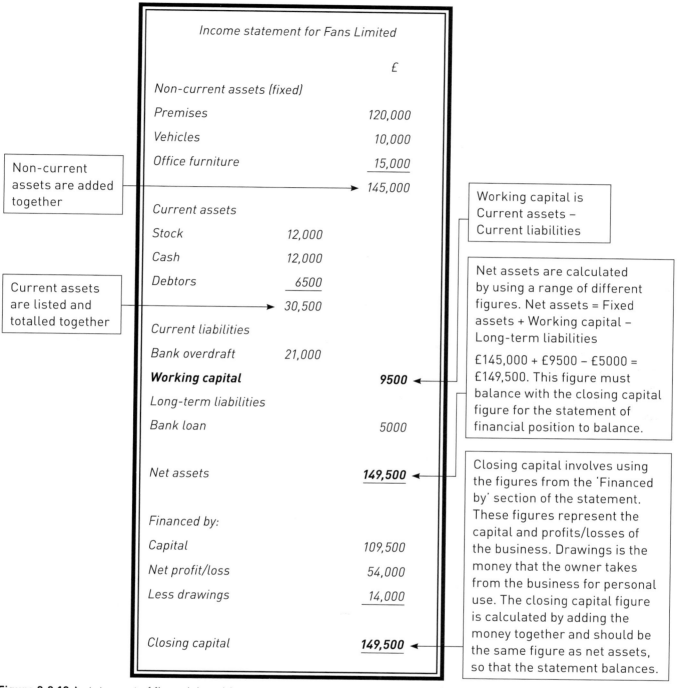

**Non-current assets are added together**

**Current assets are listed and totalled together**

Income statement for Fans Limited

| | £ |
|---|---|
| **Non-current assets (fixed)** | |
| Premises | 120,000 |
| Vehicles | 10,000 |
| Office furniture | 15,000 |
| | 145,000 |
| | |
| **Current assets** | |
| Stock | 12,000 |
| Cash | 12,000 |
| Debtors | 6500 |
| | 30,500 |
| | |
| **Current liabilities** | |
| Bank overdraft | 21,000 |
| **Working capital** | **9500** |
| Long-term liabilities | |
| Bank loan | 5000 |
| | |
| Net assets | **149,500** |
| | |
| **Financed by:** | |
| Capital | 109,500 |
| Net profit/loss | 54,000 |
| Less drawings | 14,000 |
| | |
| Closing capital | **149,500** |

Working capital is Current assets – Current liabilities

Net assets are calculated by using a range of different figures. Net assets = Fixed assets + Working capital – Long-term liabilities

£145,000 + £9500 – £5000 = £149,500. This figure must balance with the closing capital figure for the statement of financial position to balance.

Closing capital involves using the figures from the 'Financed by' section of the statement. These figures represent the capital and profits/losses of the business. Drawings is the money that the owner takes from the business for personal use. The closing capital figure is calculated by adding the money together and should be the same figure as net assets, so that the statement balances.

**Figure 2.3.13** A statement of financial position

## Activity

Balance is a small business that specialises in fitness. It has been operating for two years, during which time the business has grown.

| Fixed assets | | Current liabilities | |
|---|---|---|---|
| Premises | £1000 | Creditors | £440 |
| Fixtures and fittings | £670 | **Long-term liabilities** | |
| **Current assets** | | Bank loan | £100 |
| Stock | £450 | Capital | £1012 |
| Debtors | £156 | Profit | £900 |
| Cash | £76 | Less drawings | £100 |

- Using the figures above, prepare a statement of financial position for Balance, remembering that it should balance!
- What does the net assets figure show us?
- Why is the statement of financial position document useful to a business?
- True or false: Debtors will be found within the capital section of the statement of position.
- Why would shareholders be interested in this document?

## Key word

**Ratios**: Calculations that enable a business to judge how it is performing.

# 3.2.4 Ratio analysis

**Ratios** enable a business to judge if it is performing to the expected level, or is below or outperforming this level. Over time, the figures can be analysed and trends identified that can be used when planning for future years. Ratios do have their limitations, however. While they can identify where performance is poor, they do not give the reasons why. Ratios also do not enable a seasonal business to take into account the time of year (this information would be in a cash flow forecast).

Ratios are very useful for individuals and organisations that have a vested interest in the business. The business's managers will use the ratios to look at past results to decide how to control the business and plan for the future. Any person who is interested in investing in the business will want to see these figures, to help them decide if the business is worth investing in. Banks that have loaned the business money will want to know if it will be able to afford to repay the loan or if it is a risk.

There are two main different forms of ratio analysis that you will need to calculate and understand: profitability ratios and liquidity ratios.

## Profitability ratios

Profitability ratios involve looking specifically at whether a business has the capacity to make a profit. There are three main ratios that are used: net profit percentage, gross profit percentage and return on capital employed.

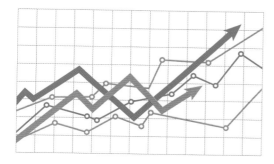

**Figure 2.3.14** Business performance

### Net profit percentage

The net profit percentage involves the net profit figure and the sales revenue. The higher the percentage a business achieves, the better, as a higher number shows it is making more profit.

$$\text{Net profit ratio} = \frac{\text{Net profit}}{\text{Sales revenue}} \times 100$$

For example:

$$\frac{\pounds 4000}{\pounds 80,000} \times 100 = 5\%$$

This means that for every £1 of goods the business sells, it makes 5% net profit, which is 5p.

A business wants its net profit ratio to keep increasing, year on year, because this shows that its profits, losses and expenses are being controlled within the correct levels, so it can continue to grow. If any reductions occur, such as the ratios reducing, the reasons should be investigated. It could be, for example, that the business had to employ extra staff or increased its advertising because it launched a new product or service, which increased the business's expenses.

## Gross profit percentage

The gross profit percentage involves comparing the gross profit and sales revenue figures. As for the net profit ratio figure, the higher the figure, the better the business is performing.

$$\text{Gross profit ratio} = \frac{\text{Gross profit}}{\text{Sales revenue}} \times 100$$

For example:

$$\frac{£30,000}{£120,000} \times 100 = 25\%$$

This figure means that for every £1 of goods the business sells, it makes 25% gross profit.

If the gross profit ratio dramatically reduces from one year to another, the business would be advised to look at the differences between the buying and selling prices of its products or services. It may be because there have been increases in the costs of raw materials within the sector, which have increased the production costs of the business. This would cause the gross profit, and the gross profit ratio, to fall.

## Return on capital employed

The return on capital employed (ROCE) ratio is a calculation that shows a business's profit, compared to the capital the owners have invested into the business. It is an important ratio, as it measures how the business is performing in its sector. The higher the ratio, the better the business is performing. If the ROCE figure reduces, businesses would be advised to investigate why this has occurred. It could be a sector-wide reduction. For example, if a bookshop's ROCE increases by just 5% from one year to another but other bookshops have similar reductions, then investors can see if this is good in comparison with the others.

$$\text{Return on capital employed} = \frac{\text{Profit before tax and interest}}{\text{Long-term capital employed}} \times 100$$

For example:

$$\frac{£120,000}{£599,000} \times 100 = 20\%$$

This figure shows what the company gets back for the money it invests, so in the above case it gets 20% back in profits. The higher the percentage, the better for a business.

# Liquidity ratios

Liquidity ratios enable a business to determine if it is able to pay its bills. They focus on a firm's current assets and current liabilities. There are two main ratios that are used: current ratio and acid-test ratio.

## Current ratio

The current ratio focuses on how much working capital a business has, meaning its liquid resources that cover its running costs (such as paying bills). Remember, if a business is short of working capital, it may have cash flow problems and would need to address this.

$$\text{Current ratio} = \frac{\text{Current assets}}{\text{Current liabilities}}$$

For example:

$$\frac{\text{£34,000}}{\text{£21,000}} = \text{£1.62:1}$$

The above answer shows that there is £1.62 of current assets. This is given as a ratio in relation to £1 of current liabilities, so is written as 1.62:1. This ratio enables a business to judge its performance. This ratio is positive, meaning the business can cover its costs. Businesses in general want to aim for a current ratio of 2:1, that is £2 of current assets to £1 of current liabilities.

The ratio, however, will be determined by the business sector. For example, internet-based businesses have different current ratios to the high street shops. This is because internet sales have increased year on year for several years, resulting in several large high street businesses ceasing trading as they were not as relevant.

If a business's current ratio figure is below 2:1, it could show that the organisation has inadequate levels of working capital. A business that has a high current ratio should consider investing the money into other opportunities.

## Acid-test ratio

The acid-test ratio uses the current assets and current liabilities, which can be found on the statement of financial position. Businesses aim for a ratio of 1:1, as this shows the organisation is able to pay its current liabilities from its liquid assets.

As with the current ratio, the ratio depends on the sector the business operates in, as some sectors enable an organisation to operate with a lower acid-test ratio than others. For example, businesses in the technology industry may have times when their acid-test ratios are very high because of high sales due to new products. For this industry, it can be difficult to balance investment into new technological developments to the sales of products. In the construction sector, a business may appear to be positive but it often takes time for accounts to be settled, which impacts on the performance of the business. A construction company would need to be aware of this.

$$\text{Acid-test ratio} = \frac{\text{Current assets less stock (closing inventory)}}{\text{Current liabilities}}$$

For example:

$$\frac{\text{£81,000}}{\text{£75,000}} = \text{£1.08:1}$$

## Activity

A market stallholder had a successful year last year and made a sales revenue of £80,000. It cost the stallholder £10,000 to purchase their stock. Other costs and expenses were £30,000. Therefore their gross profit was £80,000 – £10,000 = £70,000. Their net profit was £80,000 – £10,000 – £30,000 = £40,000.

- Use these figures to work out the gross profit ratio and the net profit ratio.
- What do these figures mean for the business?

An IT consultancy business wants to work out its current ratio as well as its acid-test ratio. Use the following figures to calculate its current and acid-test ratios:

- Current assets = £500,000
- Stock = £25,000
- Current liabilities = £310,000

## 3.2.5 Cash flow management

Managing a business's cash flow is an important aspect of financial control. We learned earlier in this section about the cash flow forecast and how this is calculated. This important document can show an organisation if it will have enough cash in the future to keep running the company, as well as ensuring that the business owners plan for the future. Businesses evolve over time and having such information enables the owners to look at the financial evidence of how the organisation is performing. This could be presented to future investors or financial institutions that may be approached to invest in the business or loan it money.

Cash flow can limit a business, as an estimate of how it will perform in the year ahead could result in incorrect assumptions being made by managers, for example regarding sales. If a business is reliant on the summer weather (e.g. a deckchair-hire business) and the weather is poor, its estimates of sales could be very inaccurate. Weather cannot be predicted but it can have a direct impact on the cash flow of a business. Other impacts could be the economy or competition from other businesses. An increase in the minimum wage will affect all businesses and may adversely affect cash flow. Businesses based in the UK are unsure how leaving the EU (Brexit) will affect them and are having to make decisions based on assumptions or predictions, which may or may not be accurate.

## Activity

You are planning a party for a relative as they have an important birthday this year.

- Write down a list of things that will be required to ensure that they have a memorable night of celebrations with friends and family. With a partner, devise some ideas for how you might budget for this celebration.

- In the same pairs, consider how a business may budget for the launch of a new product or service. What might the business need to do in order to ensure the launch is successful?

Share your ideas with the rest of your class.

## Cash inflow

In the activity above, you identified what a person may have to do to plan a birthday celebration, as well as a business planning the launch of a new product. Planning is key in both these situations, and this is the same for a business that wants to improve its cash flow position. Ideas that a business may use include:

- A company would be advised to ensure that all debtors are regularly paying bills owed to the business. If these organisations are chased and the balances are paid, this will have an immediately positive impact on the business as these payments will now be part of the business.

- A business may also want to consider reducing the amount of credit that it gives to other businesses, meaning reducing the amount of goods that another business can purchase on credit and pay for at a later date. This will also have a positive impact on the business's cash flow.

## Cash outflows

A business can improve its cash outflows in the following ways:

- A business will have to look at its cash outflows. It could request to delay paying any trade payments until others have settled their accounts with the business. This means if the organisation has purchased goods from Business A, it could ask Business A for an extension to settle the account. It could also ask Business A if it could pay off the goods over a longer time period, as this would reduce its cash outflows.

- A business could delay purchasing non-essential items that it had planned, such as machinery or vehicles, until cash flow is more fluid. At times, organisations have to reduce their spending to enable saving to recover. Delaying the purchase of assets is a method of reducing outflows.

- A business may also need to reduce the wages and salaries of its employees, or even the number of staff it employs. This would be very unpopular with staff, but if it meant that the business could work with a reduced number of staff, it would be more economical and could enable the business to be more efficient.

Businesses should be encouraged to have a contingency fund built into their cash flow forecasts. This means that if unseen circumstances occur, these can be covered by the extra fund that has been saved by the business. If businesses do not have a contingency fund, they may choose to seek additional sources of finance if cash flow issues occur. Options could be getting a loan from a bank or setting up an overdraft facility as a short-term solution. A business may also choose to enter into a **hire purchase** agreement. This is when it hires a piece of equipment or machinery for an agreed time period, paying for its use during this time. At the end of the agreement, the business has the opportunity to purchase the item or to give it back. This is why it is called hire purchase, as the item is hired with the option of purchasing it.

## Activity

- What is the purpose of a cash flow forecast?
- Identify **two** cash inflows to a business.
- Identify **three** cash outflows from a business.
- How can a business improve its cash flow management?

## Case study

Sarah Khan started a successful sandwich delivery business five years ago, as she saw a gap in the market. Her customers work on business parks and she and her team provide sandwich lunches directly to businesses using a pre-order service. Sarah has worked hard to produce all the required accounting

documents to enable her to track her finances. She has noticed over the past six months that her sales have started to decrease. This is impacting on her cash flow and Sarah is now having to consider what to do next in order to keep operating.

Answer the following question:

1  Write an email to Sarah that explains how she could investigate exactly when her sales started to reduce, offer some suggestions for research and also what she could do to improve her cash flow management.

## Remember

- Liabilities are debts the business has; assets are the different resources that the business owns.
- Fixed costs remain the same, whereas variable costs change with the level of output.
- Break-even can focus a business on the output it needs to sell in order for all costs to be covered before profit is made.
- The performance of a business can be measured using ratios but it is important to consider the sector that the business operates in when using these ratios to assess the financial position of the business.
- A cash flow forecast is a prediction of what may happen within a year for a business.

## Test yourself

1 What is the difference between gross and net profit?
2 True or false: Fixed costs do not change according to the level of output.
3 Write a definition of break-even.
4 Why is ratio analysis helpful to a business?
5 Why is cash flow management important to a business?

## Read about it

https://entrepreneurhandbook.co.uk/grants-loans – Details of the different types of grants available to businesses.

www.moneyadviceservice.org.uk/en/articles/crowdfunding--what-you-need-to-know – Information on the different aspects of crowdfunding.

www.bbc.com/bitesize/guides/zhm6sbk/revision/1 – Revision materials looking at financial records.

www.tutor2u.net/business/reference/finance-cash-flow-forecast – Explanation of how cash flow forecasts work.

www.tutor2u.net/business/blog/qa-how-does-the-acid-test-ratio-differ-from-the-current-ratio – Explanation of acid-test and current ratios.

# Learning outcome 4: Understand business and enterprise planning

## 4.1 Planning

Planning is an important aspect in all areas of life. If you want to do anything, then a certain amount of time will need to be spent making the plans, before they are put into place.

Business planning is also an essential tool, in order to successfully start or maintain the running of a business. At first it can be complex as well as time-consuming, but with careful planning, the process does get easier.

### 4.1.1 Purpose of business planning

Why do we need to plan? Monitoring a business's performance and progress is the role of its owners or managers and this can only happen with proper planning. Unless plans are made, it is very hard to know whether a business is performing to its expected levels. Initially, setting the company's aims and objectives gives the organisation focus. Aims and objectives change throughout the life of a business, but initially these may be quite simple, such as to survive the first 12 months of trade. Specific objectives give a business clear direction. Objectives should be **SMART**:

- **Specific:** State what should be achieved.
- **Measurable:** Have a measuring tool to decide if the objectives have been achieved.
- **Agreed:** Have aims and objectives that everyone involved understands and agrees to.
- **Realistic:** Be achievable in terms of the competition and market.
- **Time-bound:** Be monitored by a time frame, which should be achievable.

Ensuring that objectives are SMART and that aims can be met makes it easier for the business to make plans. Examples of aims and objectives could be:

- achieving specific sales targets
- increasing market share
- reaching a production target
- making a specific amount of profit
- breaking even in the first year.

The key elements in business planning involve four main areas: meeting personal development needs; obtaining funding and finance; operational planning; and obtaining external support.

### Activity

In pairs, discuss the stages of going on a holiday.

What do you need to think about before you get in the car or on a train, coach or aeroplane to go to your chosen destination and enjoy your time away? Write a list of what needs to happen.

Share your list with your class.

**Figure 2.4.1** Business planning

**Figure 2.4.2** SMART targets

### Key word

**SMART objectives:** Specific, Measurable, Agreed, Realistic and Time-bound objectives.

## Personal development needs and operational planning

All businesses have to plan for the future. If an organisation does not keep up with changes, it may end up closing. This has been the case for several large businesses in the past few years. Planning how a business operates is crucial for its continued success. Planning enables a business to review its current position and if changes are realistic and then to decide the process. Operational planning involves all functional areas, as any changes will have a knock-on effect on other areas.

For example, a garden business is looking to expand its staff in preparation for a busy spring and summer of selling garden furniture. It needs a designer and production and sales staff. The human resources function within the business is important for the planning stages. Forecasting the staff required for a business to fulfil its objectives is hard, but without staff input, customer orders might not be fulfilled, which would have a negative impact on the business. Once decisions have been made about staff numbers, the manager needs to make several decisions to ensure the plans can be fulfilled. These decisions include:

- the number of new staff required
- what types of contracts are required
- the job roles
- the training period, especially if specialist equipment will be used by these new job roles
- the wages/salary for each individual.

Employing new staff could also mean that bigger premises are required as the business expands, which would have a financial implication. The organisation would need to consider if it could afford this by reviewing its finances. Bigger premises would mean an increase in bills for the new building, such as electricity, gas, insurance, etc. The list of changes goes on and on. This clearly demonstrates that any operational change can impact dramatically on the business, so it is important that change is planned.

Some individuals who have worked for the business for a period of time may have the opportunity to apply for promotions within the company. If this is the case, they will need training in their new roles. Any form of training takes time and the role will not be being completed fully while the training takes place; the business will need to be aware of and make the required arrangements for this. This could mean the individual who completed the role in the past continues during the time of training and then hands over the responsibility once the new person has successfully completed all the training.

It is important staff have training opportunities to develop their skills and knowledge. By being offered training, staff feel valued and motivated to keep working hard for the business. Training needs to be appropriate and offered at the correct time, however, if it is to benefit both the organisation and the individual.

## Obtaining funding and finance

Funding and finance is one of the key elements of planning for any business, as without this an organisation will not be able to determine how much finance is required to start and keep running successfully. We have seen in Section 3.1.1 the range of different funding methods. Some of these will be more appropriate for one business than another. When providing finance for any organisation, lenders need to be convinced that the money will be repaid, and therefore it is important that they can see how capable the business will be in paying the money back. This can be achieved by:

- having a realistic plan for the business
- providing assets, such as a house, to secure any loans
- using the owner's money as part of the funding for the business
- understanding how cash will flow in and out of the business
- identifying potential sales and profits to be made
- having evidence of completed market research
- providing and demonstrating the determination, skills and communication required to make the business a success.

These different aspects will be detailed in a document called a business plan (see Section 4.1.3). Investors will want to see this document before providing any form of finance to a business.

## Obtaining external business support

Successful businesses will have completed detailed research and often have identified a gap in the market that their business idea could fill. The TV programme *Dragons' Den* is a good example of showcasing different ideas, with individuals presenting or pitching their business ideas to a panel of potential investors and highlighting their product's or service's unique selling point (USP).

### Activity

Watch an episode of *Dragons' Den*.

- Write notes on the different products/services that are featured on the episode, the information the people gave in their pitches and the outcomes from the potential investors. Did anyone want to invest and, if so, what was the offer and was it accepted?

**Figure 2.4.3** Pitching a business idea

- Using your notes, write a blog on your opinions of the episode of *Dragons' Den* you watched, to inform others about the programme.

If a business has support from other organisations or businesses it might be able to secure finance quicker, which could mean it moves from the planning stages to the business operating stage at a faster rate. Some local authorities offer external support in the form of mentoring, where a business is put in contact with an established business individual who can provide help and support for the business. They could provide help with market trends, competition, research, etc. Mentors may offer a different viewpoint on the research an individual has produced, or identify errors that have occurred. They will not complete specific work but will point the business in the right direction so it can complete the necessary work to begin operating. The business may retain the mentor for several months or until it feels confident to operate fully on its own. Having a mentor enables an organisation to seek advice and support, to hopefully ensure a successful start to the business.

The government website shows the support that is provided in most areas of the country, in terms of finance and business support for people who are wanting to start a business: www.gov.uk/business-finance-support

---

**Activity**

Oxfordshire Business Enterprises Ltd (OBE) is an organisation that offers free advice to business start-ups in Oxfordshire: http://oxonbe.co.uk

Another website, called the Growth Hub, offers similar support to businesses in the south-west of the country: www.heartofswgrowthhub.co.uk

- Research both websites to discover what they can offer individuals.
- Report your findings back to the rest of your class.

---

## 4.1.2 Benefits of business planning

The benefit of having a clear vision for a business is that the people involved can plan for the future. If issues occur, staff will know that these have been thought through and contingency plans have been made, so that the business can continue to be successful. Sadly, this is not the case for some organisations and in the past few years some companies have ceased to trade. This was often because they had not kept up with changes in the markets. For example, Toys 'R' Us was reliant on customers going to their large shops, which were often in out-of-town retail parks. With the increase in internet sales and with rival businesses offering cheaper deals on goods, sales at Toys 'R' Us started to fall and it appeared not to be able to compete. The business had to maintain the high rents and bills for the retail shops, compared to internet companies that just have to have suitable warehouses with staff to store the stock and the ability to deliver the products to customers. Overall this is cheaper, which is why lower prices and special offers can be given to customers. By contrast, Toys 'R' Us had to charge more. Toys 'R' Us had not seen how the changes could impact on its business and did not plan effectively, resulting in it ceasing to trade in 2018.

There are four main areas that highlight the benefits to a business of planning:

- supporting the bidding process
- managing change
- finance strategies
- identifying potential problems.

## Case study

Mike wanted to set up a florist in his local town, as he had always had a passion for gardening, plants and flowers. There were no other florists in the local town centre and his only competition would be from a flower stall at the local market that visited once a week on a Thursday. Mike had no business knowledge and did not know how to go about setting up a business. He had saved some money that he could put towards starting his business, but he knew that this would not be enough to get it up and running.

He approached a business support group called the Business Hub to Help (BHH) and was allocated a business adviser. The business adviser met with Mike on several occasions and asked him at the end of each meeting to prepare some documents for the next session. Initially, the business adviser asked what Mike's overall aims and objectives were for the business and where he wanted to be in two years' time. This made Mike think about the future and what he wanted to achieve.

One week Mike was asked to research the competition within a 20-mile radius. Another week he was given different financial options that he could access, but he had to work out which would be the most appropriate for his business. The options were discussed at a meeting and Mike's adviser was able to offer some good advice. It was decided a business loan would be most appropriate, with Mike using his house as an asset to secure the loan. His business adviser also suggested that Mike should consider setting up a website. Mike had not considered this idea, so he investigated the viability of setting this up for another aspect of his business.

Flowing Flowers has now been operating for 18 months and has proved to be successful. Mike is the manager of the shop and he employs three assistants. The shop is busy and has started to supply flowers for weddings, funerals and other events. Some venues recommend Flowing Flowers to their clients, which boosts sales. Flowing Flowers stocks a range of seasonable flowers, but in the future is looking to also stock a variety of house plants and unusual plants to appeal to a range of customers. Mike says that BHH really helped him with his ambition of opening a successful florist.

Answer the following questions:

1 What does BHH do?
2 How do you think that BHH helped Mike move forward with his business idea?
3 What specific advice did BHH give Mike?
4 Why do you think that organisations like BHH are vital for new business start-ups?

## Supporting the bidding process

Any new business, or one that has been trading for a short amount of time (one to two years), will be trying to get known in its own right, to compete effectively in different sectors. A business needs to get its name known for the right reasons so it is able to pursue the different directions it may take. A business may start one way but two years later be operating in a different way, which had not been considered before. For example, a business may start with a retail shop but if most of its trade is completed online it might close the shop and concentrate on online sales only.

Having a good business plan will enable an organisation to seek new opportunities and present its ideas to potential investors. One aspect could be to bid for a new business opportunity. These are often available to small businesses and enable them to bid or pitch ideas for a large or long-term project, stating the time frames, costs, labour, etc. required to complete the work. Other businesses may bid something similar, so an organisation needs to ensure that it is competitive and can deliver on the details of the specific bid. An example could be businesses bidding to supply the food to hospitals or schools. The offers will be considered by a panel and a decision made.

There are four stages to the bidding process:

### Stage one: Prepare the bid

A business will be required to highlight how it can complete the project, focusing on the time, cost and labour required. All elements must be realistic as the reputation of the business will be at stake if these are judged incorrectly. If the deadline is not met and four more weeks of work are required, this would impact on the outcomes of the project. If discounts are given, it would be advised to highlight these within the bid, providing the business can fulfil them. Remember that successful bids are not always the ones with the lowest costs. The quality of the bid is taken into account, which is why business planning is a crucial aspect of bidding.

### Stage two: Submit the bid

It is important that the bid is submitted correctly, for example that deadlines are met. If it has to be submitted using a specific platform that the business has not used before, it must research this to ensure it is familiar with it so the bid can be successfully submitted on time. Any issues could damage the work that has been put in to creating the bid before it is even read!

### Stage three: Present the bid

If its bid gets through the first stage, the business may be requested to present its ideas to a panel. This would be an opportunity to meet with the people involved in the panel, either in person or via an online meeting. Businesses should be prepared to answer a variety of questions about the documentation that has been submitted and any adjustments that are required can be completed at this stage.

### Stage four: Successful bid notified

The successful bid will be notified, so it is important that the business is aware of the date when this will happen. For the successful organisation, the next stage will be to start work so it can deliver on what it promised. If a business's bid is unsuccessful, it is appropriate to ask the panel for the reasons why. This may be brief, but any feedback will benefit the organisation for future opportunities that involve the process of bidding.

| Stage 1:<br>Prepare<br>the bid | Stage 2:<br>Submit<br>the bid | Stage 3:<br>Present<br>the bid | Stage 4:<br>Successful<br>bid notified |

**Figure 2.4.4** The bidding process

The process of bidding is a formal process for a business to present what it can offer compared to its competitors. It can give an organisation new opportunities to complete business in a way that it may not be able to on its own, and also provides new opportunities for the future. Successful businesses do not stay the same and often look ahead to the future, to ensure that they remain current and competitive.

## Managing change

The business world is constantly evolving. You only need to look at the changes to our shopping habits since the invention of the internet. Businesses like Amazon have changed the UK's average high street. This has impacted other businesses, and many have ceased to trade because they were no longer relevant. Businesses like Comet, Habitat, Toys 'R' Us, Maplin and Woolworths have all become victims of the internet. Other famous and established businesses such as Marks & Spencer and Debenhams are having to close specific stores, as they are just not getting the customers through the doors to make the sales that are required for them to continue operating in high streets, with their expensive rent and rates.

**Figure 2.4.5** BMW was planning to shut its plant in Cowley for one month in preparation for the UK leaving the EU

Managing changes in a business's markets is an important aspect of planning. Marks & Spencer, for example, is coping with this by closing some stores, meaning it can put the savings into other aspects of the business, such as developing new product lines or paying increasing production costs, etc. Organisations are having to plan for the UK leaving the European Union in 2019, without knowing what the final Brexit deal will be. For example, in September 2018, BMW announced that it would shut its plant in Cowley, where it makes the BMW Mini, for one month from when the UK was due to leave the EU. This was so it could ensure, if there was any disruption in getting parts, that it would be able to operate as normal when production resumed a month later.

Like Marks & Spencer and BMW, all businesses are trying to manage change. A smaller organisation could complete a **SWOT analysis**. This is a quick and easy form of assessment that focuses on the Strengths, Weaknesses, and potential Opportunities and Threats for the business. A SWOT analysis is completed using a chart like the one in Figure 2.4.6.

**Key word**

**SWOT analysis:** The Strengths, Weaknesses, Opportunities and Threats that a business may face.

|             |            |
| ----------- | ---------- |
| Strengths   | Weaknesses |
| Opportunities | Threats  |

**Figure 2.4.6** A SWOT chart

A business may, for example, identify its Strengths as having a unique product range, its Weaknesses as having a small range of customers, its Opportunities as selling goods at local pop-up shops, and its Threats as the increase in business rates and minimum wage rates for employees, which will affect its finances.

A business must plan and make provisions for changes it knows are occurring, such as Brexit, new government legislation or increasing rental charges. Listening to customers and their requests/feedback, as well as noticing changes in the markets, will impact the business. Who would have predicted ten years ago that Toys 'R' Us would cease trading?

**Activity**

In pairs, identify the different ways that your school communicates with people who have an interest in it (its stakeholders), such as parents, carers, businesses, governors, etc.

● Ask your teachers how these methods have changed in the past ten years. What is different now?

● What are the future plans for the school? Can you find any information on this? Are new buildings planned, for example?

Individually research two different businesses – one large and one small. Look on their websites for information relating to their future plans. Report your findings back to your class.

## Finance strategies

Another benefit for a business of planning for the future is the focus on ensuring that its finances remain positive, to enable it to pay bills and balance the inflows and outflows of the business. Keeping accurate records, knowing when payments have to be made and customers paying the business on time, are all important aspects of having a good understanding of financial management. We established earlier in the chapter the importance of financial documents, such as break-even, cash flow forecasts, income statements, statements of financial position and ratio analysis. All of these form the financial strategy for the business. Ratio analysis provides data that shows how the organisation is performing. Having all this information together means that if, for example, the business wants to expand its operation, it can see if this is a realistic option and the time frame in which this could occur.

## Identifying potential problems

Having a good understanding of the market that a business operates in will enable it to try to plan for potential issues that may occur in the future. Of course, a business cannot predict every problem that may occur, such as the long hot summer of 2018. This was fantastic for many businesses that rely on seasonal weather being good, but not for farmers who rely on a mixture of sunshine and showers in the UK, who lost many crops or had to harvest crops early. This hot weather impacted on the costs for this industry, which were then passed on to the businesses that rely on these goods, which in turn passed the costs on to customers. This weather could not have been predicted. Climate changes throughout the world are impacting on costs to both business and customers.

Other potential problems that a business should focus on include staff illness, as this can have an immediate impact on the operation of a business. Power failures can also impact on operations, particularly for businesses that are reliant on technology – which most are these days for communication alone! Natural disasters such as flooding or fire can be disastrous for an organisation. For example, if businesses know that they are positioned near a flood plain, then suitable planning should be made in case this situation occurs. If stock is stored there, an alternative storage location in a different area could be sought. Having such plans in place means that even if the business is flooded, the stock is safe.

An organisation could ask itself certain questions:

1 When, why, where and how might the identified risks occur in the business?
2 Are the risks internal to the business? (Risks inside the organisation can be managed by the organisation, such as staff sickness.)
3 Are the potential problems external to the business? (Problems outside of the organisation include changes to the taxes it has to pay.)
4 Who might be involved in this problem?
5 Who might be affected by the issue?

A business could also consider a variety of different 'What if' scenarios, which is when the organisation focuses on what it would do if something happened. For example, 'What if there was no access to the internet or our suppliers suddenly went out of business?'

Businesses could also think about the worst-case scenario that could happen. This might seem a little dramatic, but it makes the organisation focus on what to do if such a crisis should unfortunately occur. This helps it deal better with smaller situations and hopefully keep positive!

For example, a business delivers food to individuals. The main modes of transport it uses all break down in the same week as they were not maintained well because it was too costly for the business at the time. As a result, all the business's prepared food has to be thrown away and customers do not receive their orders. Customers then leave bad reviews of the company and it makes the national press.

This example of a bad situation could have been avoided by the transport being maintained, as the expenses to keep the vehicles running would have been far less in the long term, compared to the loss of money from the wasted food and the loss of business resulting from the negative publicity. Considering potential problems that could occur enables a business to analyse the likelihood and the consequences of them actually happening, so that situations can be managed effectively if they do occur.

## Activity

Look at the following image of a naturally-occuring problem that could affect a business.

**Figure 2.4.7** A sinkhole

Sinkholes in the UK seem to be reported more frequently and can occur after heavy rainfall. Advise an organisation how it should plan for such a situation, which could affect all aspects of its business – from deliveries to the premises, to customers being unable to access the business when the road is shut to be repaired.

## 4.1.3 A business plan

A **business plan** is a formal document that details how the organisation will operate and succeed. A business plan will detail:

- the financial aspects that are required in order for the business to function, which include where the funding will come from and how much it needs to operate
- the market that the business will operate in
- the resources that are required to make the products or services
- the marketing required
- how the business will be managed/organised
- the overall aims and objectives for the business.

The document will be read by potential investors, so it is important it is clear and ensures the reader is fully aware of all aspects of the business. It should answer all of the questions that the reader had prior to reading the business plan.

A business plan will follow a particular order: company description; market analysis; marketing; people and operations; financial plan.

### Company description

Section one is a company description which introduces the business and details:

- the name of the company
- a summary of the business
- its potential market sector
- its location
- its prospects.

The company description also details the aims and objectives and the structure of the business and its legal status. This first section is important, as the reader will use it to decide if they want to find out more about the organisation. If the business idea does not interest the potential investor, they may not continue to the next section.

### Market analysis

Section two is based on a market analysis of the business's products or services. It is a chance for the organisation to describe:

- its main target market, which is the people or companies the products or services are aimed at
- how it can compete in the chosen market(s)
- the predicted growth of the market(s)
- its potential suppliers and why it has chosen them
- the profile of the industry that it will be entering.

The business plan may also state if patents or copyright are required. This is relevant if the organisation needs to protect its product so that other businesses do not use the same idea. This section is more specific than the company description section, as it focuses on how the business hopes it will compete in the market.

## Marketing

Section three details the marketing of the business using the 4 Ps – Product, Price, Place and Promotion. Further descriptions are included within each section of the 4 Ps. This part might detail what the unique selling point (USPs) is for each of the products or services. It also contains information regarding market research that has been completed, and the distribution channels that will be used so the customers or suppliers get the products or services they have ordered. This section also has details of the different promotional methods that will be used. This may include examples of promotional materials, as well as figures relating to the overall costs of producing the products compared to the selling prices.

## People and operations

Section four is based on the people involved and the operations of the business. The business plan describes how the organisation is structured and managed, with a breakdown of the number of employees required to run the business. It details the different managers and how many staff they are responsible for, so that investors can get an overall understanding of how the business will be run.

This section has information about the production processes that will make the products or services, as well as the equipment and material requirements. It also includes the business's quality control procedures. See Unit 01 Section 3.1.3 for more on quality control.

## Financial plan

The final section of a business plan is the financial plan. This part of the document details the required start-up costs and the running costs of the business, as well as the break-even calculations. It also contains information regarding the income statement, which will include the gross and net profit figures and the forecast statement of financial position, as well as any plans for growth and development in the future.

Having five sections to a business plan enables a variety of investors to focus on different elements. An investor could be a business with different specialists within the firm who will look at the document. For example, the marketing director would have more specific knowledge for the marketing section than the finance director, who would be more interested in the financial plan section.

**Activity**

Write an article that details why it is important to complete a business plan if you want to gain finance from any form of financial institution. Give examples where you can.

## Remember

- Organisations can access business support using local advisers who can be mentors to new business start-ups.
- Business planning enables an organisation to plan for a variety of situations that may occur, which could be internal or external to the business.
- There are five different sections to a business plan.
- A SWOT analysis can form part of a business plan.
- A business plan will be read by potential investors who may want to invest in the business.
- Business planning demonstrates the business's vision and details how it will achieve this vision.

## Test yourself

1 What is the role of a business adviser or business mentor?
2 Why would a business bid to be part of a new project?
3 Why do businesses produce a business plan?
4 Identify the **five** different sections within a business plan and write a sentence to describe each section.
5 Who will be most interested in the details of a business plan?

## Read about it

www.businessballs.com/strategy-innovation/business-planning-and-marketing-strategy – Tips on preparing a business plan and marketing strategy.

www.heartofswgrowthhub.co.uk – Advice on how to start and grow a business.

https://smallbusiness.chron.com/five-steps-bidding-process-23870.html – Outlines the steps in a bidding process.

www.princes-trust.org.uk/help-for-young-people/tools-resources/business-tools/business-plans – Advice from the Prince's Trust on writing a business plan.

www.princes-trust.org.uk/help-for-young-people/tools-resources/business-tools – Further business advice from the Prince's Trust.

## Assessment practice

Sixty per cent of your final mark for this qualification will be based on a synoptic project set by NCFE. The tasks in this section will enable you to practise your skills in preparation for your final assessment. This practice assessment focuses on the knowledge, understanding, skills and techniques that you have been learning in this qualification. It is important that you read all the details carefully and then attempt all parts to gain the most practice.

## Scenario

One year ago you started a sandwich and panini delivery service to companies based in business parks on the outskirts of your town. There are no other businesses in your area offering this service. Customers order their lunches via an app and payment is also taken at the time of the order. The delivery van used is small and uniquely decorated by you.

Your business has proved very popular and after a year of trading you have decided to expand. In order for this to happen, you will need to purchase another delivery van as well as employ more staff so that an efficient service can continue. You also need to increase your advertising as in the past you have relied on word of mouth and social media. You have decided that a bank loan would be the best way to fund this expansion to your business.

You currently work on your own, but will need to employ someone on a full-time basis to help with ordering the fresh ingredients and preparing the lunch orders. You will also need a new delivery driver to deliver the orders to several business parks each day, with you covering the other business parks. You will complete the marketing,

monitor the orders, and organise the finances and the new staff of the business, as well as preparing and delivering the orders. Luckily, you like being busy!

You need to prepare a detailed business plan that gives potential investors all the information they need, and which you hope will persuade them to invest in your business. The five different sections of your business plan will be: company description; market analysis; marketing; people and operations; and financial plan.

Several documents have been produced in your first year of trading that you will need to use as part of the financial part of your business plan.

| Income statement | £ |
|---|---|
| Sales revenue | 180,000 |
| Less cost of sales | 30,000 |
| **Gross profit** | **150,000** |
| | |
| Less expenses | |
| Wages and salaries | 35,000 |
| Rent | 5000 |
| Operating licence (for business parks) | 1000 |
| Vehicle | 5000 |
| Repairs and maintenance | 3000 |
| | 49,000 |
| | |
| **Net profit** | **101,000** |

**Statement of financial position**

|  | £ | £ |
|---|---|---|
| Fixed assets |  |  |
| Premises |  | 50,000 |
| Machinery |  | 1000 |
| Vehicles |  | 10,000 |
|  |  | 61,000 |
| Current assets |  |  |
| Stock | 2000 |  |
| Debtors | 1000 |  |
| Prepayment of insurance | 1000 |  |
| Cash | 3000 |  |
|  | 7000 |  |
| Current liabilities |  |  |
| Trade payables | 1000 |  |
| Accrual of rates | 1000 |  |
|  | 2000 |  |
| Working capital |  | 5000 |
| Long-term liabilities |  |  |
| Bank overdraft |  | 5000 |
| Net assets |  | 61,000 |
| Financed by: |  |  |
| Capital |  | 50,000 |
| Owner's funds |  | 13,000 |
| Less drawings |  | 2000 |
|  |  | 61,000 |

**Cash flow forecast figures:**

Opening balance is £10,000

Cash inflows for the 12 months are £6000 (average)

Cash outflows for the 12 months are £3000 (average)

Complete a plan of how you will complete this assessment. Your plan should include the tasks that you have to complete, as well as the dates by which you will complete each task so that you can move on to the next part of the project. By planning your work you will ensure you give yourself time to complete everything by the deadline. Some sections may take longer, so make sure you show this within your plan.

1 Write a description of your business and how successful it has been in the first year of trading. Provide some details of what your business supplies to customers.

2 You deliver to business parks – why does this work? You now know that there is demand for this service on other business parks, but how do you know this? What are your plans for your expansion? Explain all this and more in the market analysis section of your business plan.

3 Provide some examples of the marketing that you intend to do if your business loan is successfully granted, and provide some costs for this.

Customers currently order on an app, but could there be other methods that you might want to think about?

4 So far you have been running the business on your own, but now you have recognised that you will need more staff to help you manage the expanded business. In the people and operations section of your business plan, describe how many new staff are needed and why, as well as what tasks they will complete as part of their jobs. Will you be in charge?

5 The final part of the business plan is the financial aspects. You need to put together a cash flow forecast as well as explaining what the figures from the income statement and statement of financial position show. You could use ratio analysis to show how successful the business has or has not been over the past year.

Your completed business plan should be handed to your teacher on or before the deadline date.

# Glossary

**Aesthetics**: How a product looks or feels.

**Analysis**: Studying the results of an investigation to help come to a business decision.

**Annual percentage rate (APR)**: The amount charged in interest to a customer who has taken out a loan.

**Assets**: Resources that a business owns so that it can operate.

**Break-even**: The point at which a business makes no profit and no loss. It is the point at which total costs equal total revenue.

**Business insurance**: When a business pays a company to provide compensation in case anything happens to it or to its employees or customers when completing its business activities.

**Business plan**: Aimed at investors such as banks, who may invest money into a business.

**Cash flow**: The movement of money into and out of a business.

**Cash flow forecast**: A prediction of what may or may not happen within a year for a business, by predicting the flow of money coming into and out of the business.

**Chain of command**: The line of communication and authority within a business.

**Competitive pricing**: Setting a price that is similar to that of a local competitor.

**Competitors**: Businesses that produce or sell similar products.

**Contract of employment**: A formal document with both the employee and employer agreeing to the terms and conditions.

**Contribution**: The amount left over after variable costs have been taken away from sales revenue. Contribution per unit is calculated as selling price per unit less variable cost per unit.

**Crowdfunding**: When many different people give money, often for the purpose of starting a new project.

**Customer base**: The main customers who access a business's products and services.

**Customer retention**: The ability of a business to keep its customers.

**Customer/market segmentation**: The division of a market into groups or segments.

**Demand**: Supplying customers with the products and services that they want.

**Digital manufacturing**: Applying digital technologies to the manufacturing process.

**Discrimination**: When a person is favoured over another.

**Diversification**: A method that businesses use to break into new markets by developing and selling new products.

**Entrepreneur**: A risk-taker who sets up a business or businesses with the aim of making large amounts of profit.

**EPOS**: Electronic point of sale; used to check stock levels.

**Equipment**: The tools or machinery required for a business to produce its products or services.

**Extension strategies**: Actions a business can take to extend the life of a product and increase sales.

**External growth**: Business growth by buying or taking over other businesses.

**External recruitment**: When a business recruits and employs a new person to the business who has the skills, knowledge and experience required for the job role.

**External training**: When employees go to a location outside of the workplace and receive training from external trainers.

**Fittings**: Items that can be moved around a room or business premises, such as chairs, desks, cabinets.

**Fixtures**: Items in a business that are fixed to the wall or floor so they cannot be moved.

**Focus group**: A group of people who participate in a discussion about products and services.

**Franchise**: A business where the franchisor (the owner of the business idea) grants a licence (the franchise) to another business (the franchisee) to operate its brand or business idea.

**Function**: The job for which a product was designed; any product must be able to perform its function.

**Functional area**: A department that plays a specific role within an organisation and whose employees carry out a particular aspect of the work of an organisation.

**Funding**: A method of gaining finance for a business.

**Geographical expansion**: When a business increases in size and requires additional premises.

**Grant**: Funding provided and supported by the government to help small businesses.

**Hire purchase**: When a business hires a piece of equipment or machinery for an agreed time period, paying for its use during this time. At the end of the agreement, the business has the opportunity to purchase the item.

**Horizontal integration**: When a business combines with an established or similar organisation operating in the same area of industry.

**Income statement**: Details the revenue (the money) that comes into a business from the sale of products or services, as well as the expenses that the business has used.

**Innovation**: Bringing new ideas to the market.

**Intellectual property law**: Protects a business's products, the designs it creates, its brand name or inventions.

**Interest**: An amount of money that is added on to a loan and must be repaid by the customer.

**Interest rate**: The amount that a customer is charged for taking out credit. It is often calculated as a percentage and over the duration of the finance, e.g. 28% APR.

**Internal data**: Data and information held by a business.

**Internal growth**: How a business has grown from where it originally started to the current time and where it strives to be in the future.

**Internal recruitment**: When an existing employee gains a new role within the same business – often a promotion.

**Internal training**: When employees receive training at the business location, from trainers who are either from the business or come into the business.

**Invention**: The creation of new items.

**IT infrastructure**: The hardware, software, facilities and networks that a business uses to enable information to flow.

**Joint venture**: When two businesses join together for the purpose of completing a long- or short-term project.

**Legal requirements**: Laws that a business must comply with, otherwise it will face fines or closure of the business.

**Liabilities**: Debts that a business may have incurred while trading.

**Limited liability**: When the business owners are liable only up to the amount of money they have invested in the business.

**Loan**: A method of gaining finance from a financial institution. The loan must be repaid with interest within an agreed amount of time.

**Loss leaders:** A pricing tactic in which a business is willing to make a loss on a particular product in order to get customers to purchase the product.

**Market**: A place where buyers and sellers come together to interact and exchange goods with each other.

**Market-orientated business**: Produces goods based on customer wants and needs.

**Market research**: The actions of a business to gather information about customers' needs and wants.

**Market share**: The section of a market controlled by a particular business.

**Merger**: A form of external growth for two businesses that voluntarily decide to become one organisation.

**NFC reader**: Near-field communication readers, also known as contactless payment, are used to take payment from customers for items they purchase.

**Partnership**: A business that is owned and controlled by two or more individuals.

**Patent or copyright**: Provides legal ownership of original pieces of work.

**Premises**: Where an organisation operates its business.

**Price penetration**: Introducing a product at a lower price than usual to attract customers, then gradually increasing the price over time.

**Price skimming**: Introducing a product at a high price, then gradually lowering the price over time.

**Primary (field) research**: Gathering data and information that has not been collected before.

**Product lifecycle**: Traces the journey of a product from its development and launch to its removal from sale to the public.

**Product-orientated business**: Produces only goods that it is good at making.

**Profit**: A financial gain. It is calculated as the difference between the total revenue and total costs.

**Promotional pricing**: A business tactic in which the price of a product is reduced in order to attract the attention of customers.

**Prototype**: A model of an initial design of a product, which can be altered before being produced for customers to purchase.

**Psychological pricing**: Setting a price that appears attractive to a customer.

**Qualitative data**: Information about people's opinions and views.

**Quality control**: When a business checks that its products and services meet the required standards, so that customers will be satisfied when they purchase them.

**Quantitative data**: Factual information that is collected, for example information about customers' ages.

**Ratios**: Calculations that enable a business to judge how it is performing.

**Raw materials/goods**: Natural resources that are turned into products and services.

**Research**: A method of finding out information on an aspect of business.

**Risk**: Something that may harm any individual who has dealings with a business.

**Risk assessment**: A formal document that businesses complete to assess the risks of a particular situation.

**Secondary (desk) research**: Gathering data and information that has already been collected.

**SMART objectives**: Specific, Measurable, Agreed, Realistic and Time-bound objectives.

**Sole trader**: A business that is owned and controlled by one person.

**Stages of recruitment**: The different processes that a business goes through to ensure it employs the right person for an advertised job role.

**Statement of financial position**: A snapshot of a company's assets and liabilities at a particular point within the financial year.

**SWOT analysis**: The Strengths, Weaknesses, Opportunities and Threats that a business may face.

**Takeover**: When a business acquires control of another organisation.

**Target market**: A particular group of customers at which a good or service is aimed.

**Transport**: The methods a business uses to move (transport) products to customers.

**Unique selling point (USP)**: The key product feature that separates a product from its competitors.

**Unlimited liability**: When the business owners are personally liable for the debts of the business in the event that the business cannot pay them.

**Vertical integration**: When a business that operates in one part of an industry acquires another business in the same industry but that operates at a different level within the supply chain.

# Answers to Test yourself questions

## Unit 01 Introduction to business and enterprise

### 1.1 Entrepreneur (page 5)

1 Entrepreneurs are individuals who spot a gap in the market, develop a business idea and are willing to take risks in order to make the idea a reality. These individuals are usually highly motivated to become successful.

2 Invention involves the making of new items. Inventors design and make products that are not currently available for sale.

  Innovation is how these new ideas are brought to the market.

3 A willingness to take risks: Any new business venture carries risk, regardless of how carefully planned and researched the business idea is. A successful entrepreneur will be willing to invest large amounts of money and time into their new ideas, while being fully aware that customers may reject the project and that it could ultimately fail.

  An ability to undertake new ventures: Entrepreneurs usually have vast amounts of imagination to identify business opportunities to fill gaps in the current marketplace.

  A desire to show enthusiasm and initiative to make things happen: Entrepreneurs do not wait for something to happen. They will show determination, drive and energy to launch the new business.

  Resources and funding: Entrepreneurs need these to make the investment to set up a business.

  Time and commitment: Entrepreneurs need to understand and calculate the risks and potential rewards that could occur from a venture.

  The ability to invent and innovate: Invention involves making new items. Inventors will design and make products that are not currently available for sale.

4 In order for an entrepreneur to be successful, they need to have a new idea that stands out from the rest of the market. As a risk-taker, the entrepreneur needs to have the courage to put their idea into the marketplace.

### 1.2 Business aims and objectives (page 13)

1 The aim of most businesses is to make a profit. Some organisations, however, for example charities, exist to provide a service and are classified as not-for-profit organisations. Sports clubs may also be non-profit-making and exist to provide services to their members. A new business will struggle to make a profit in its first few years of trading, therefore new businesses usually aim to break even.

2 Non-financial aims and objectives are those that help improve an organisation as a whole.

3 Market segmentation is the splitting of a market into smaller segments.

4 The main non-financial aims and objectives of a business include:
   - customer satisfaction
   - expansion
   - employee engagement and satisfaction
   - diversification
   - ethical/corporate responsibility.

5 Customer retention is the ability of a business to keep its customers.

### 1.3 Structures (page 21)

1 A franchise is a business where the franchisor (the owner of the business idea) grants a licence (the franchise) to another business (the franchisee), so it can sell its brand or business idea. The franchisor owns the business idea and decides how the business will be operated and run.

2 A sole trader is a business owned and controlled by one individual, whereas a partnership is an organisation owned and controlled by two or more individuals. In most cases there are between two and

twenty partners, however this number can be exceeded for professional partnerships, e.g. accountants and solicitors.

3 Unlimited liability means the sole trader would need to pay the business's debts if they could not be paid.

4 Answers could include:
- sale of shares to family and friends
- debentures
- mortgages
- loans
- bank overdrafts.

5 Consumer co-ops: Members buy goods in bulk, sell to other members, and divide profits between members.

Worker co-operatives: Workers buy the business and run it; decisions and profits are shared by members.

Producer co-operatives: Producers organise distribution and sale of products themselves.

## 1.4 Stakeholder engagement (page 24)

1 A stakeholder is any individual who has an interest in a business.

2 Internal stakeholders are those within an organisation, for example owners, managers, employees and workers.

External stakeholders are those outside an organisation, for example customers, suppliers, shareholders, the local community and the government.

3 The stakeholders of a school/college include teachers, parents, students, governors, government, senior leadership team, site supervisors, pastoral staff, etc.

## 2.1 Marketing mix (page 45)

1 Some businesses develop a unique selling point (USP). This is a feature that separates a product from its competitors. There are a number of examples of products with identifiable USPs in the market today, for example:
- car performance, e.g. BMW, Porsche
- branding, e.g. Nike
- design, e.g. Apple.

2 Any product must be able to do the job for which it was designed – this is known as the function.

A product must be financially viable and cost effective to produce. Not all products can be made out of gold or silver; rather, materials appropriate to the product need to be used. Ensuring appropriate manufacturing costs is known as economic manufacture.

Aesthetics (how a product looks or feels) is very important when trying to sell goods or services. For example, luxury cars often have a leather interior to create a luxurious feel.

3 The main sections of the product lifecycle are:
- Development: A business researches and develops the product before it is made available for sale.
- Introduction: The new product is launched on the open market. The product is advertised to improve customer knowledge and to encourage sales.
- Growth: Customers are now familiar with the product and sales increase. At this time, the number of sales increases at its fastest rate and profits rise.
- Maturity: Sales of the product have reached their highest. It is likely that the number of new customers is reducing and growth is limited. Other businesses may have entered the market.
- Decline: Sales of the product begin to fall. Customers are no longer interested in the product and may have switched to newer alternative products.

4 Advertising: Businesses may produce new advertisements for their product.

Price changes: A business may decide to put up or reduce the price of its product.

5 In general terms, a business will price its product by working out what it costs to buy or make the product and then adding the amount of profit it would like to make. There is little point in selling a product for a lower price than it has cost to produce – the business would make a loss.

6 Competitor pricing occurs when a business sets a price that is similar to that of a local competitor.

7 The clothing retailer could use:
- Leaflets as they are low-cost and can be targeted to customers in the local area.
- A website to advertise its products – it could choose to:
  - place adverts on search engine results pages
  - pay for pop-ups (small internet windows that appear over the top of web pages and are used to attract attention)
  - place adverts on social networking sites.
- A newspaper – it would need to decide whether it wanted to advertise in national newspapers, local newspapers or free newspapers. Free and local newspaper advertisements are relatively cheap, whereas large adverts in national newspapers are extremely expensive. Small businesses tend to focus on free and local newspapers to keep costs down and to target the customers that are likely to purchase their products.

8 Sales promotion techniques include:
- Buy one, get one free: A discount offered to customers who purchase multiple items from the business.
- Competitions: Businesses often offer prizes in competitions to encourage customers to purchase a product.
- Point-of-sale material: A promotional tool used where the product is sold. In supermarkets, this is often by the tills. There may be large displays to promote the products.

## 2.2 Market research and markets (page 54)

1 Market research is a vital part of any business success. It involves finding out information about the market in which the business operates.

2 Interviews, observations, questionnaires, focus groups and consumer trials.

3 Gender, occupation, income, geographic, lifestyle.

4 Segmentation ensures customer needs are matched and met. By focusing on one particular area, businesses are more likely to meet the needs and wants of their customers. Customers are more likely to purchase goods and therefore the business's sales will increase.

When a business ensures it focuses on its customers, it is more likely that customers will keep returning to the business for their purchases. This leads to increased customer retention.

Market segmentation allows for targeted marketing, as a business is able to deliver its marketing and advertisements to customers who have an interest in the product being offered.

As the business knows which segment of the market to target with its marketing, the right customers are reached and lower marketing costs are incurred. With careful monitoring and targeting of appropriate customers, there is the potential for an increase in market share.

5 To understand the market and to reduce risk: Comprehensive market research allows a business to understand the needs of the market and then to provide goods and services to meet those needs. By developing a working knowledge of customer needs and wants, the business reduces the risk of making inaccurate decisions about products or services.

To gain customers' views and understand their needs, and to aid decision-making: By understanding customer needs and wants, managers can make informed decisions. Market research allows customers to discuss their views, needs and wants, etc., in terms of products and services offered.

To inform product development and to promote the organisation: Comprehensive and accurate market research reduces the risk when launching new or updated products. Whenever a business launches a new product, there is a possibility that customers will not want to buy it. The business can reduce this risk by completing appropriate research, as it will be aware of what customers are looking to purchase in the future.

## 3.1 Operations management (page 59)

1 Continuous flow production. This is similar to mass production, except that in continuous flow operations the production line operates 24 hours a day, 7 days a week. This reduces the costs of stopping and starting production. Very few workers are required and the majority of the work is completed by machine.

2 In batch production, small quantities of identical products are made. This method also uses machinery and manpower. The products tend to be relatively expensive due to the labour costs. Every batch will be slightly different.

3 Lean production is a management approach that aims to cut waste. At the same time, the business focuses on high quality. The idea is used throughout a business, from design to distribution.

4 When organisations grow, they are often not able to complete all of the business tasks themselves. They need to outsource some of their operations, meaning that another business is hired to do some of the work. For example, payroll operations, IT operations or website design may be outsourced.

Small businesses, for example sole traders, also outsource various aspects of their business as they do not have all of the necessary skills available to do the work themselves.

The outsourced work is usually of high quality but is considerably more expensive than if it were completed in-house.

5 Benchmarking is the continuous, systematic search for and implementation of best practice, which leads to superior performance. The use of benchmarking aids a business in maintaining and improving quality.

Businesses that benchmark measure their performance against that of other organisations and aim to learn from the best firms in the world.

Businesses use benchmarking to assess the:

- reliability of products
- ability to deliver items on time
- ability to send out correct invoices
- time taken to produce a product.

## 4.1 Customer service and internal influences and challenges of growth (page 63)

1 Customer service is the way in which a business looks after its customers.

2 Good communication skills for interacting with customers; patience to understand customers' needs and wants; attention to detail (it is important that employees focus on customer requirements); good product knowledge; excellent personal presentation (employees need to be appropriately dressed and act in a manner that attracts and retains customers).

3 Effective customer service will:

- provide word-of-mouth promotion
- improve business reputation
- encourage repeat business
- set the business apart from its competitors
- provide brand awareness
- ensure customer loyalty and encourage customers to purchase from the business in the future.

## 4.2 Internal influences (page 69)

1 A functional area is a department that plays a specific role within an organisation and whose employees carry out a particular aspect of the work of the organisation.

2 The marketing department promotes or advertises the organisation's products and services. The aim is to target customers and ensure they are fully aware of what the organisation offers.

3 The operations department deals with the production processes within a business. It is responsible for overseeing, designing and controlling how production processes work.

4 Answers may include:

- Planning how many staff may be needed in the future, often referred to as 'manpower planning'.
- Preparing all the paperwork for a job vacancy – adverts, job descriptions, person specifications.
- Determining wages and salaries.
- Recruiting and selecting employees.

- Providing training and development for all employees.
- Being responsible for employee welfare and motivation.
- Dealing with employee complaints or grievances.
- Implementing organisational policies, for example health and safety.
- Dealing with dismissals and redundancies.

5 The finance department organises and allocates financial resources, reports on financial performance, and monitors cash flow.

## 4.3 Internal challenges of growth (page 71)

1 As a business grows, it benefits from a reduction in average costs of production. This is known as 'economies of scale' and is what gives larger firms a competitive advantage over smaller firms.

2 The largest firms often benefit from external economies of scale. These include setting up local supplier firms, often in competition with one another, which reduce buying costs and allow the use of systems such as just-in-time. Also, local colleges will set up training schemes suited to the largest employers' needs, giving an available pool of skilled labour.

3 Answers may include:
- Purchasing: As firms increase the size of their orders for raw materials or components, the cost to purchase each individual component falls. The firm gets bulk discounts on the larger orders, which reduces the average cost of production.
- Technical: As businesses grow, they are able to use the latest equipment and incorporate new methods of production. This again reduces average costs of output.
- Financial: As firms grow, they have access to a wider range of capital, reducing the cost of borrowing for investment. Also, as the assets grow, businesses are able to offer more security for borrowing, reducing the risk to the lender and therefore reducing the cost of borrowing.
- Managerial: As businesses grow, they are able to employ specialist managers.

These managers know how to get the best value for each pound spent, whether it is in production, marketing or purchasing. This reduces the cost of output.
- Advertising: As firms grow, each pound spent on advertising has greater benefit for the firm.

4 When diseconomies appear, the average costs of production rise with output.

Diseconomies include problems with communication – as a firm grows and levels of hierarchy increase, the efficiency and effectiveness of communication can break down. This increases inefficiency and therefore raises average costs. It may be harder to co-ordinate, satisfy and motivate workers in larger firms. This means they do not give their best, so average output falls and average costs increase. These diseconomies of scale are often qualitative in nature and hard to measure financially, but they still reduce the efficiency of the business. As organisations grow in size, they can become increasing difficult to control. For example, businesses may need to deal with traffic congestion, the breakdown of relationships with suppliers and buyers, competition for labour and increasing employment costs.

## 5.1 External influences (page 77)

1 During a recession stage, customers have very little money to spend on luxury goods, so businesses will need to consider developing cheaper products.

During a growth period, customers have more money to spend and are likely to want to purchase new goods or services. Businesses will therefore develop and sell new products.

On reaching the boom period, customer spending is at its highest and businesses will introduce and sell a wide range of new products.

During a decline period, businesses suffer from a decrease in sales and there is little or no demand for new products or services. A business will be unlikely to develop new products during this time.

# Unit 02 Understanding resources for business and enterprise planning

## 1.1 Business research (page 87)

1  Research is an important aspect of business as the results can give a person who wants to set up a new enterprise information about their potential customers, whom their competitors could be, the potential demand for their products or services, and the legal requirements that they will need to fulfil in order to set up their business.

2  The customer base for a nursery shop will be parents, family members who may want to buy gifts for the baby/child, and friends who also may purchase gifts.

3  Answers may include: There are newsagents that sell newspapers, magazines, snacks, drinks, tobacco products and books, as well as a few toys for children. Charity shops that sell clothes, shoes, second-hand books, toys and games, as well as new cards and stationery. An express supermarket that sells a variety of raw and cooked meats, bread, dairy products, frozen food, fresh fruit and vegetables, toiletries, snacks, drinks.

Newsagents and supermarkets compete with each other as they sell some of the same products, although supermarkets sell a bigger range of products. Charity shops stock mainly second-hand items so will not be in direct competition with the other two businesses.

4  A shop like Tesco will research the population of the area that it serves and make an estimate of how many products the people will purchase. It will look at the figures from the previous year to help it predict the sales that will be made. If required, it could request stock from other local stores if they have spares available. Any leftover stock could be shared with other stores or sold at different times of year, for example New Year.

5  It is the law, so that if a business enterprise is not abiding by UK laws, it will face fines and potential prosecution from the authorities. There is no choice.

## 1.2 Resource planning (page 94)

1  Raw materials are natural resources that are turned into other products and services, such as wood to make a dining room table.

2  Fish, flour (breadcrumbs) and egg, and trees to make the packaging.

3  Near-field communication (NFC) readers, also known as contactless payment, are a method of payment for a customer, whereas an EPOS (electronic point of sale) system is used in retail outlets to check the levels of stock.

4  Businesses use and apply digital technologies to the manufacturing process, which in turn makes the production process quicker, meaning that the business is more efficient.

5  The three different parts are the hardware, the software, and the facilities and networks that a business uses to enable information to flow.

## 1.3 Business growth (page 98)

1  A method that businesses use to break into new markets, which means that they can develop and sell new products.

2  To increase the size of the business and compete effectively in the market.

3  Horizontal integration is when a business combines with an established or similar business operating in the same area of industry. Vertical integration is when a business that operates in one part of an industry acquires another business that is involved in the same industry but at a different level within the supply chain.

4  Two businesses might join together for the purpose of completing a long- or short-term project.

5  A takeover is when a business acquires control of another business. It is happening more frequently because some businesses are struggling, for example due to changes in shopping habits, meaning that businesses are being taken over so they can continue to trade.

### 2.1 Human resources (page 116)

1  A job may arise because of expansion of the business, because an employee retires, because an employee gains an internal promotion, or because an employee leaves the business.

2  Shortlisting.

3  Four stages: verbal; written; final written; dismissal.

4  Internal training generally happens within the business. External training happens outside of the company, at another site and by trainers who are not employed by the business.

5  Permanent, temporary, fixed-term, part-time, full-time, zero-hours contracts.

### 3.1 Business and enterprise funding (page 121)

1  Answers may include:

- Personal savings: Savings that the owner of the business invests in the business.
- Bank loan: An amount of money that is borrowed from a bank with an agreed pay-back date. The bank earns money, called interest, in return for lending the money to the business.
- Credit card: Enables a customer to purchase items on credit, and then each month the customer is notified of the amount of credit that has been used. This should then be paid back or interest will be added on to the amount each month.
- Loan from family and friends: This is when a business is funded by friends and family of the owners. Like a bank loan, it is money that is borrowed for a period of time but this will be agreed with the parties involved.
- The Prince's Trust: Supports new businesses with start-up loans of up to £5000. Like other loans, the amount will be paid off monthly, with agreed interest for the duration of the loan.
- Grants: These are supported and funded by the government. The government enables small businesses that meet specific criteria to apply for grants of between £500 and £500,000.
- Credit agreements: When any form of credit funding is taken out by a business, an agreement of the specific details (also known as the terms and conditions) will be documented, with both parties being given copies of the document. It will detail the amount of credit, the duration of the credit, the interest to be charged, what will happen if payments are not made, etc. It is a legally binding document.
- Business Angels: These are often individuals who have wealth and an entrepreneurial mind, who are willing to take risks in order to own a proportion of a business. They effectively give money to invest in a new business venture, in the hope that success will follow.
- Overdrafts: This is a short-term source of finance and it is when a bank allows a business to withdraw money from its account up to an agreed amount even if it does not have the balance in its account.
- Crowdfunding: This involves many different people giving money, often for the purpose of starting a new project. People donate small amounts of money, normally using the internet, which can generate publicity for the new project or business as more people give money.
- Trade credit: This is when credit is given to a business for an agreed amount of time, such as 30, 60 or 90 days. The balance must be paid within the agreed timescale.

2  Once the savings have gone, the individual will have no money left to survive on, especially if the business does not succeed.

3  An overdraft is a short-term financial arrangement that has an agreed limit, which is often small. A bank loan is a larger amount of money that will be paid off over years rather than months, with an agreed APR.

4  When many different people give money, often for the purpose of starting a new project.

5 The Prince's Trust.

It was set up to improve the lives of disadvantaged young people in the UK.

6 When any form of credit funding is taken out by a business, an agreement of the specific details (also known as the terms and conditions) will be documented, with both parties being given copies of the document. It will detail the amount of credit, the duration of the credit, the interest to be charged, what will happen if payments are not made, etc. It is a legally binding document.

## 3.2 Business and enterprise finance (page 143)

1 Gross profit is the figure that is calculated using the money that is coming into the business, for example from sales revenue. Net profit is the figure calculated once expenses have been taken off the gross profit figure.

2 True

3 Break-even is when Total revenue = Total costs.

4 Ratio calculations enable a business to judge how it is performing.

5 It shows a business if it will have enough cash in the future to keep running the company, as well as ensuring that the business plans for the future.

## 4.1 Planning (page 156)

1 To help a non-business specialist start up a business and provide help and support to get the organisation up and running.

2 It would enable a small business to bid or pitch its idea for a large or long-term project, stating the time frames, the costs, the labour required, etc., to complete the work. These opportunities could expose the business to new markets and to potential openings for the business.

3 To detail in five different sections the aims and objectives for the business and how it intends to achieve them. These sections are: company description; market analysis; marketing; people and operations; financial plan.

4 Section one is a company description which introduces the business and details the name of it, a summary of the business, its potential market sector, the location and the businesses prospects.

Section two is based on a market analysis for the products or services that the business will operate.

Section three details the marketing of the business using the 4 Ps – Product, Price, Place and Promotion.

Section four is based on the people and operations of the business. The business plan describes how the organisation is structured and managed, with a breakdown of the number of employees required to run the business.

The final section is the financial plan. This part of the document details the required start-up costs and the running costs of the business, as well as the break-even calculations, the income statement (which will include the gross and net profit figures), and the forecast statement of financial position, as well as any plans for growth and development in the future.

5 Investors who may contribute financially to the business.

# Index

advertising 31, 35, 38–42, 70
aims 6–13, 64, 144, 154
analysis 83–4, 151, 154–5, 158
annual percentage rate (APR) 118
appraisals 65, 112
assets 126–7, 134–6, 139
banks 22–3, 118, 120
benchmarking 57
bidding process 149–50
Boston Matrix 33
brand image 25, 26
break-even 6–8, 127–30, 155
business growth 10, 60–3, 94–8
    challenges 69–71, 76
business insurance 86
business plans 154–8
capital 69, 134–5, 138–9
cash flow 9, 10, 65, 131–2, 140–2
cash flow forecast 130–2, 140, 142, 158
change management 145, 150–1
communication 5, 71, 92–3
competition 32, 36–7, 62, 73–5
competitive pricing 37, 38
competitors 36, 50, 83–4
consumer protection 75, 90
consumer trials 50
continuous flow 58
contracts of employment 105–6
copyright law 75
corporate responsibility 12
costs 3, 6, 35, 121–6, 155
    fixed 6, 124–6, 128, 129
    running 124, 169
    start-up 124, 169
    total 6–7, 127–8, 129
    variable 6, 7, 125, 128
crowdfunding 120
customer bases 82, 85
customer needs 11, 46, 64
customer retention 62, 162
customer service 60–3, 70
data types 46–7
debtors 126–7, 141
decision-making 46, 62
delayering 20
demand 35, 85–6
design 27, 32
digital manufacturing 92
disciplinary action 108
discrimination 108
diseconomies of scale 70–1
distribution channels 34
diversification 11–12, 94–5
e-commerce 35
economic cycle 73–4
economic manufacture 27
economies of scale 36, 70
electronic point of sale (EPOS) 90–1
employees 22, 23
    appraisals 65, 112
    development 65, 108–13, 145–6
    engagement/satisfaction 11
    and planning 155, 158
employment 66, 73–4, 75
entrepreneurs 2–5
equality 107–8
ethical issues 12
expenses 121–3, 133
extension strategies 30–2
external influences 72–7
finance 3, 63–5, 117–43, 146
    aims/objectives 3–9

and business growth 69–70
    concepts and calculations 121–3
    funding 22–3, 117–21, 146
    planning 154, 155, 157–8
    strategies 152
financial documents 121–3, 127–36, 152, 155, 157–8
flat organisations 18–19
focus groups 49
franchises 15, 17
function 27, 32
functional areas 63–4
funding 22–3, 117–21, 146
geographical expansion 95
government 13, 22, 50
Health and Safety 65–6, 75, 87
Herzberg, Frederick 67
hierarchies 18–19
horizontal integration 95–6
human resources 63, 65–7, 99–116
hygiene factors 67
income 12, 35, 36, 76
income statement 121–3, 133–4, 155, 157
innovation 4, 23, 32–3
intellectual property law 86–7
internal influences 60–71
interviews 103
invention 4
IT infrastructure 93
job advertisements 99–103
joint ventures 97
just-in-time (JIT) 55
kaizen 56
lean production 55–6, 165
legislation 13–17, 35, 75, 86–7, 90, 105–8
liabilities 126, 134–6, 139
liability 86
    limited 14, 16, 17, 20
    unlimited 14, 16, 163
loans 118–19, 168
location 12, 25, 32–5, 155
loss 121, 122, 133
management 22, 23, 70
market analysis 154–5, 158
market research 45–54, 82–7
market segmentation 11
market share 29, 32
market-orientated 53
marketing 44, 63, 154, 155, 158
marketing mix 25–54
markets 11, 32, 45–54
Maslow, Abraham 66–7
Mayo, Elton 67
mergers 96
motivation 3, 4, 66–7
near-field communication (NFC) 89–90
needs
    customer 11, 46, 64
    theory of 66–7
objectives 6–13, 64, 154
    SMART 144
observations 49
operations 55–9, 63, 67–9, 145–6, 155
organisational structures 18–21
outsourcing 55, 165
ownership 16–17, 22–3
partnerships 13–14, 16, 20, 22
patent law 75
pay 72, 113–15, 141–2
payment systems 89–90
place 12, 25, 32–5, 155
planning 144–58

price 25, 31, 35–8, 123, 128–9, 155
    equilibrium 36
price penetration 38
price skimming 37, 38
pricing strategies 31, 36–8
primary (field) research 47–50, 51, 62
Prince's Trust, The 119
private limited companies 13–14, 16, 17, 20
private sector 13–17
product 25, 26–33, 155
product development 32–3, 46
product lifecycle 29–33
product-orientated 53–4
production types 55–6, 58, 92
profit 3, 6, 8, 36, 121–2
    gross 122, 133, 138
    gross profit percentage 138
    net 122, 133, 137
    net profit percentage 137
profit margins 36
profit maximisation 9
profit sharing 115
profitability 8–9, 137–8
promotion 25, 38–46, 64, 155
promotional pricing 37, 38
prototypes 92
psychological pricing 37, 38
public limited companies 13, 16, 17
public sector 13
qualitative 46
quality 12, 57
quantitative 46
questionnaires 47–8
ratios 136–40
recessions 73–4
recruitment 65, 99–108
redundancy 20, 108
remuneration 72, 113–15, 141–2
research 47–50, 50–1, 62, 82–7
resources 88–94, 154
restructuring 20–1
return on capital employed (ROCE) 138
revenue 3, 6–7, 9, 121, 123, 127–9, 133
risk 2–4, 46, 86–7
sales revenue 122, 123
secondary (desk) research 50–2, 62
shareholders 14, 16, 17, 22, 23
social media 39
sole traders 13–14, 16, 20, 22
stakeholders 21–4, 134, 136
start-ups 99–116, 124
statement of financial position 134–6, 155, 158
stock 85, 125
substitute goods 35, 36
supply 22, 35
support, business 146–7
surveys 47–8
SWOT analysis 151
takeovers 96–7
tall organisations 18–19
taxation 35, 75–6
technology 70, 73, 89–94
total quality management (TQM) 57
trade credit 120, 141
training 65, 109–11, 145–6
transport 88–9
trends/fashions 35, 73
unique selling points (USPs) 26, 155
vertical integration 96
wages 72, 113, 141–2
working capital 135, 138–9